I0198368

Hosea

Spokesman of Heavenly Love

Robert F. Simms

© 2023 by Robert F. Simms

All rights reserved. No part of this book may be reproduced in any form without permission in writing from the publisher, except in the case of brief quotations embodied in critical articles or reviews.

Unless otherwise indicated,
all quotations from Scripture are from
the King James Version.

ISBN: 978-1-7378117-2-5

Printed in the United States of America

Abbreviations Used

Bible translations referred to in this book generally employ the abbreviations shown below.

NIV	New International Version
NLT	New Living Translation
ESV	English Standard Version
BSB	Berean Study Bible
KJV	King James Version
NKJV	New King James Version
NASB	New American Standard Bible
AMP	Amplified Bible
CSB	Christian Standard Bible
HCSB	Holman Christian Standard Bible
CEV	Contemporary English Version
GNT	Good News Translation
ASV	American Standard Version
DRB	Douay-Rheims Bible
GWT	God's Word Translation
ISV	International Standard Version
NET	New English Translation
WBT	Webster's Bible Translation

Contents

INTRODUCTION

Hosea is the first book of twelve "minor prophets" in what Jews collected during the second-temple period of their history — what is often referred to by Christians as the inter-testamental period. The tag of "minor" refers to the relative length of the writing compared to the "major" writings of Isaiah through Daniel. The name "Hosea" in Hebrew means "salvation," and would translate to the modern English name "Joseph," as well as being linguistically similar to "Joshua" and "Jesus." In fact it was Joshua's original name before Moses renamed him (Numbers 13:16). "Hosea" or one of its variants was a popular name throughout Jewish history, reminding people of the historical revelation of God to his people, in which he was their Savior.

Hosea the man

We know nothing of Hosea himself outside this writing. The first verse of Hosea gives the name of "Beeri" for his father, but other than a reference to a Hittite named Beeri in Genesis 26, no other Beeri is reported in the Bible. Some personal details about Hosea's immediate family are garnered from the text of the book itself. He married and fathered three children. His wife, Gomer, was described as "a wife of harlotry" (1:2), and at the instruction of the Lord he gave his children names that were not-so-cryptic messages to Israel, as the forthcoming exposition will detail.

Setting

Internationally, the time of Hosea's ministry was during the rise of Assyria as a major world power, about 783-687 B.C.. World figures of the day included Tiglath-Pileser III, the first of the new Assyrian kings, Hoshea of Israel, and fellow prophet Isaiah, a contemporary of Hosea. Other prophets (in Judah) included Micah.

Israel was in political decay and moral ferment. Amid moral

turpitude at home, there was the growing threat of takeover from abroad. While the social trend was a shift to Baal worship with its fetish for prostitution, the country's leaders were scurrying around having summit meetings with the superpowers, trying to line up friends in an uncertain political climate.

Hosea's ministry was in his homeland of Israel, the northern kingdom. Internal evidence suggests that he lived in the northern part of that kingdom as well. His locality did not restrict the scope of his preaching, however: In 1:1 he mentioned the kings of Judah — Uzziah, Jotham, Ahaz and Hezekiah—as well as Jeroboam of Israel. This served the purpose of dating his prophecy (as below) but also implicitly identified the political personalities who were about to be implicated in the crimes and sins God's message would address:

- In 1:7 Hosea relayed God's intentions of saving Israel without need of armies.
- In 1:11 Hosea foresaw an ultimate reunion of the southern and northern kingdoms.
- In 4:15 God's message wooed Judah not to share in Israel's sins.
- In 5:5, Hosea declared that in spite of God's wooing and warning, Judah was taking the same path as her northern brother, and in 5:8-15 Hosea viewed the prophecy of war between them.
- In 6:4, God wooed Israel and Judah together.
- In 6:11 and 8:14 he warned Judah by itself about its sins and their inevitable judgment.
- In 11:12 and 12:2, Judah's punishment was in view in the prophet's message.

So the message of Hosea, while having the priority purpose of speaking to the sins of Israel and God's coming judgment, reached out to the southern kingdom and implicitly pled for unified repentance, while envisioning certain punishment when repentance was not forthcoming.

This wider scope of Hosea's target audience raises the question of whether it was a merely technical inclusion of Judah or if there were some method by which his message reached into the southern kingdom. For instance, could portions of what eventually became what we know as the book of Hosea have been circulated not only in Israel but in Judah by some planned outreach?

Date

Hosea gives us enough information to date the years of his ministry within a few years. In 1:1 he tells us he was active during the reigns of four of Judah's kings:

Uzziah reigned from about 783-742 B.C.
Jotham was king from about 742-735 B.C.
Ahaz reigned from about 735-715 B.C.
Hezekiah was king from about 715-687 B.C.

The problem with this date range when applied to Hosea is that it places the beginning of Hezekiah's reign after the date of the northern kingdom's fall to Assyria in 722 B.C. This would almost certainly invalidate Hosea's own statement that he was still prophesying in Israel during at least some of the reign of Hezekiah.

Whatever the solution with regard to dating the southern kingdom's regents, Hosea also tells us that Jeroboam son of Joash was king of Israel during his ministry. The dates of Jeroboam's reign were about 786-746 B.C., and following him were several kings who succeeded by assassination and intrigue until the fall of Samaria in 722 B.C. Most scholars believe that Hosea's ministry ended a year or two before Samaria's overthrow under Sargon of Assyria. So it is possible that Hosea's entire ministry lasted sixty years or so.

Why Hosea did not, in 1:1, identify the royal houses of Shalum, Menahem, Pekah and Hoshea—which followed Jeroboam—as coinciding with his years of preaching we cannot know for certain. However, it may be simply that by the time Jeroboam died of natural causes and was succeeded by Zachariah, who reigned for only six months, the judgment of God was fully in motion and nothing Hosea or any other true prophet of God said by way of warning could stop it. The sole mention of Jeroboam, therefore, may date the period of time during which Israel had some semblance of a chance for repentance and restoration.

Author

The author of the book refers to Hosea in the third person in chapter 1, but he opens what we know as chapter 3 by saying, "The Lord said to *me,* and uses the first person once again in 3:2. The use of the third person pronoun is no proof that anyone else wrote the work, as the use of the first person is no proof that Hosea did. But the suggestion of the first person in the highly personal information given in chapter 3 is that Hosea's hand is evident in the work. In any event, the book has long been attributed to Hosea himself. We know of no subsequent "school of Hosea" that might have been responsible for it.

Especially if one posits that Hosea wrote down some or much of his prophecy during his ministry and had some method in place for the dissemination of these writings especially to Judah, it would seem even more likely that he compiled his own writing into what eventually survived as "Hosea." More likely than not, he finished the work before his probable death in 724 or 723 B.C.

Text

While the Jewish community had the work of Hosea and compiled it with the other minor prophets during the second-temple period, the work was not without textual problems. It was in a dialect of Hebrew scholars today call non-standard, and translators have always encountered difficulties with it. For instance, in the oldest manuscripts available, 4:17-19 are regarded as unclear. In 5:11, 6:7, 7:12, 7:16, 8:13, 9:13, 10:5, 10:10, 10:11, 10:13, 11:2-7, 12:4, 13:2,9-10,14-15, and 14:8, ancient translations and the standardized Hebrew of the7th century A.D. are in disagreement, or the Hebrew itself is unclear.

Part of the lack of clarity is due to the vowel pointing system of the Masoretes, which may not match the Hebrew texts that were used as the basis of the Septuagint.

Portions of Hosea are in prose and portions in poetry: 2:19-23, 11:1-4, 11:8-9, and 14:4-8, at the very least, are clearly poetic, if not the entire chapters in which those verses appear. However, as is often true of the prophets, their bent when writing was to express themselves in poetic language, even if the form—parallel lines, etc.—was not specifically poetic.

Themes

Hosea's own introduction to his book summarizes its themes in the somewhat theatrical account of his marriage to a woman who would betray him, and his having children whose names were to stand for Israel's coming encounter with God over their sins.

The themes of the book may be expressed as:

- Sin's fruits
- Sin's discovery
- God's discipline
- God's faithfulness
- God's restoration

In the text, Hosea goes back and forth somewhat in developing these themes. Possibly we may detect his stitching together some of his written records of his own preaching where the emphases oscillate.

Exposition of Hosea

Chapter 1

As with other prophetic writings, Hosea begins by introducing the reader to the prophet and giving at least terse information as to how he came on the scene. The message God wanted proclaimed was inevitably to be infused with controversy and conflict. The question of who would deliver it, therefore, was up to the authoritative calling of God.

1 **The word of the LORD that came unto Hosea, the son of Beeri, in the days of Uzziah, Jotham, Ahaz, and Hezekiah, kings of Judah, and in the days of Jeroboam the son of Joash, king of Israel.**

The first readers of Hosea's written work may well have been two generations or so after the events reflected in the writing, but still during the time of Babylonian captivity. For perspective, the modern American reader might consider thinking of American Presidents and British Prime Ministers forty years previous, when reading a work authored in that period of history. If a prophet were to arise in America today—more of one that is now in the church abroad—doubtless he would address the governments of the nation, condemning the fall of America from her spiritual heritage. What would he would say, even about leaders who have been relatively benign?

In the day of this book's writing, developments in international tension and cultural rot suggest to God's people the tremors that precede volcanic historical events. No doubt the idolatrous developments in the northern kingdom of Israel, the preaching of other anointed prophets and the study of God's previous acts would have led Hosea to suspect the end of Israel was near. But he had no need to rely on his intuition. In some way that was undeniable to Hosea, God had revealed to him what was imminent in his country's near future.

The listing of kings gives historical reference, obviously, but probably also introduces the idea that the criticisms within the book are going to be aimed in part at leadership figures of the nation, who are partly to blame for the people's spiritual condition.

2 **The beginning of the word of the LORD by Hosea. And the LORD said to Hosea, Go, take unto thee a wife of whoredoms and children of whoredoms: for the land hath committed great whoredom, departing from the LORD.**

"Wife of whoredoms" (KJV) is "promiscuous woman" (NIV), "a wife inclined to infidelity" (NASB), "woman of promiscuity" (CSB), "a prostitute" (ISV), or "wife [who] will be unfaithful" (GNT). Thus begins a passage that has been roundly debated for centuries. Did God tell Hosea to marry a woman who was already known to be an adulteress, or someone who would subsequently become one?

In answering that question, one should consider first the likely circumstances of the man Hosea at the time of his calling.

At the very first of his ministry, from the time that he was aware that God was at work upon his life in a unique way, Hosea was almost certainly dramatically impressed with the infidelity of Israel to God. Lacking information that indicates that Hosea's call came out of the blue as would be the case if he were "converted" from idolatrous living himself—we may assume that he had eyes to see and a heart to perceive, and had been led of God to understand the spiritual harlotry that was going on in his nation, so that when he realized he was picked to preach to the nation, his heart was already in it. It was in this heart, prompted and stirred by God, that he envisioned his life acting as a living message to the people around him. Not just as a good example among the evil. Not just as the voice of exhortation (which he was). But instead as a living metaphor of God's relating to his people.

Other prophets had participated in theatrical demonstrations of divine messages. For instance, under God's direction, Ezekiel had built models of Jerusalem, its wall, and enemy forces constructing siege ramps against it. Ezekiel then lay down beside it and went through a series of demonstrative actions, all of which told a story to his "audience" about the coming judgment on Judah.

Hosea's life was occasionally like this. He, himself, was always an implied message, because of the continuing circumstances in which God told him to involve himself: he told him to marry. And the person he married under divine direction made his life a continuing illustration before a sinful nation.

...wife of whoredoms...

This term, as illustrated above by varying translations, is subject to widely differing interpretation. The Hebrew is *eset zenunim,* "wife of harlotry," but knowing the original words does not solve the problem.

As already stated, some interpreters believe Hosea was instructed to marry a woman already known to be an adulteress. This interpretation does not have any textual evidence to support it, as the words "wife of harlotry" themselves give us no clue. However, this view frequently identifies Gomer as a prostitute *already* involved in the fertility cult of Baal. The function of this view is to emphasize that God knew when he called Israel that it would be unfaithful to him.

The weakness of the view is that God knew of Israel's eventual unfaithfulness even if it hadn't taken place in Israel's experience yet. And Gomer would not have had to be an adulteress yet for the image of her as unfaithful to "work" as a silent sermon when it became known. In addition, there is the problem of God's own restriction of priests marrying impure women.

The other interpretation of this key image in Hosea is that God instructed Hosea to marry a particular woman knowing that she would *eventually* be unfaithful. God knew it, of course, and Hosea knew it because God had revealed it to him. We might paraphrase: "Go marry a woman who is bound to be unfaithful to you." The Good News Translation, in fact, takes this viewpoint: "Go and get married; your wife will be unfaithful."

The advantage of this interpretation is that it doesn't require Hosea to do something that God elsewhere prohibits, and which, it could be argued, would serve no real purpose. It also accurately reflects what it symbolizes: that God took Israel unto himself in the relative purity of her initial commitment, and she later left him for other gods. (The actual events of Israel's beginnings may argue against this view, since Israel in the wilderness after the exodus worshiped golden calves.) In addition, the instruction to take an adulterous wife is paired with the mention of "children of adultery." Since the latter had not come along yet, it is natural to assume that the adulterous state of the wife was yet in the future as well.

Although the image of Hosea's being married to a fertility prostitute (future or present) was symbolic of his message about spiritual unfaithfulness, prostitution itself was rampant. There are indications that Israel had an international reputation for it. Think of some modern equivalent associations, just in the United States: New York with muggings; Chicago with murders; San Francisco with homosexuality; Las Vegas with gambling; and so on. This was the situation regarding prostitution in Israel. If the point of Hosea's "ministry" was at least in part to address the literal problem of prostitution, it was well on point.

2   ...children of whoredoms...

This term uses the same Hebrew for "whoredoms" as the previous one paired with "wife." And for the same reasons it raises interpretive questions. Just as crucial to the imagery of Hosea's marriage is the coming of children to that marriage. Are these children Hosea's by an adulterous wife; or are they actually the children of one or more of her lovers—or clients? The answer, still debatable, may be helped by further reading in the text.

The overall message of Hosea was to be illustrated by the character of his own family. God wanted Israel to see in Hosea an illustration of the Lord, and in Hosea's wife an example of an unfaithful people. When

Israel perceived what Hosea's marital and family situation was symbolic of, they would understand how much the nation's unfaithfulness had grieved God.

3   So he went and took Gomer the daughter of Diblaim...

With no details to identify Gomer, we do not know if Hosea already knew her or was providentially guided to her. We do not know, for purposes of sharpening our interpretation of her status, if she was connected already to the Baal cult. We know only that Hosea came to know she was the one God wanted him to marry and that he did so.

...which conceived and bare him a son.
4   And the LORD said unto him, Call his name Jezreel; for yet a little while, and I will avenge the blood of Jezreel upon the house of Jehu, and will cause to cease the kingdom of the house of Israel.
5   And it shall come to pass at that day, that I will break the bow of Israel in the valley of Jezreel.

As certainly as he knew to marry Gomer, Hosea knew to name his first son Jezreel. The question of how God revealed things to prophets when their own writings do not give us details is always of interest to us, if only to give us some encouragement that God will reveal his direction to us in similar ways.

Interestingly, we do not have as much problem discovering the method of revelation utilized among the patriarchs. Theophanic incidents involving Abraham, Isaac and Jacob, for instance, tell us quite clearly that "the LORD appeared" or "the Angel of the LORD appeared" to them, giving them promises and directions. After the completion of the Pentateuch, such appearances diminished but did not disappear.

By the time of the major and minor prophets, a few significant events of divine appearances seem to have taken place. Isaiah had a quite dramatic revelation (Isaiah 6:1ff). In the opening phrases of Jeremiah, that prophet tells us that "the word of the LORD came unto me" (Jeremiah 1:4). The account of Ezekiel says "the word of the Lord came expressly unto Ezekiel the priest" (Ezekiel 1:3). Jonah admits that "the word of the LORD came unto Jonah" (Jonah 1:1). Micah refers to his authority as "The word of the LORD" (Micah 1:1). —And so on throughout the Old Testament. The use of the phrase "the word of the LORD," where "Lord" is the Hebrew *Yahweh,* has been thought by increasing numbers of scholars to represent a theophany, involving at the very least a voice (awake or dreaming), and possibly an appearance such as the patriarchs had. Most of the prophetic authors themselves do not describe what their experiences were like.

The range of possibilities for the prophets' reception of the word they were to proclaim includes dreams, visions, theophanies, or merely dramatic realizations brought on by a concurrence of events. In some way that was undeniably of God, Hosea knew the name of his first son, and knew what it would mean.

It would be difficult to conceive of the purpose to be served by these children's being fathered by someone other than Hosea. **Jezreel,** in particular, is implied to be his: **"she conceived and bore him a son." Lo-Ruhamah** and **Lo-Ammi** are not so clearly identified; but on the other hand there is nothing said about their being fathered by anyone else.

The phrase **"children of harlotry"** or **"children of unfaithfulness"** (v2) appears then to mean children born to an adulterous woman, in the midst of a marriage polluted by adultery on her part. It is predictable—and entirely sufficient to God's purpose—that such children would have the cloud of suspicion over them, and their social situation would ever reflect the suspicious circumstances under which they were born.

This was the anguish and adversity under which Hosea was to preach, and it was the plan of God for him. Why would God specifically design such grief-filled circumstances for Hosea?

God's purpose was laid out very clearly in these verses: **"because**

the land is guilty of the vilest adultery in departing from the LORD." Hosea's life was to become a living metaphor for the relationship of God to a people mired in the deepest sin. He was called to accept a life of tragedy, so as to illustrate for the nation who would hear him the nature of their terrible unfaithfulness. No doubt such life circumstances were a tremendous burden for a person to bear; but with the presence and comfort of God, Hosea could accomplish it.

So that the living illustration would not be easily missed, Hosea was to give his children names that underscored the message to Israel. The first was to be **Jezreel.** God gave Hosea the reason for the name: **"I will avenge the blood of Jezreel upon the house of Jehu."**

The message inculcated in the name Jezreel needs some detailed explanation. The name called to mind the valley of Jezreel, where Jehu slew the princes of Judah and Israel, as well as Jezebel. 2 Kings 9 describes Jehu's *obedience* to the charge given him by a prophetic emissary of Elisha's, who anointed him king and told him to "destroy the house of Ahab" and Jezebel. Jehu did exactly that. He killed Joram, son of Ahab, but also killed Ahaziah, king of Judah, who had allied with him (2 Kings 9:27). Then, after having Jezebel thrown from the city wall of Jezreel, Jehu had the frightened guardians of Ahab's seventy sons in Samaria to kill them and send their heads to him at Jezreel. He then killed more friends of Judah's King Ahaziah.

In the afterglow of that slaughter, Jehu announced that he would lead Samaria in redoubled worship of Baal. At the moment, anyway, it was a deception, and when he had all the priests of Baal assembled, his soldiers followed his orders and killed them.

It is important to realize, when interpreting this phrase, "blood of Jezreel," that God had *commended* Jehu for killing the house of Ahab as instructed (2 Kings 10:30) and promised him his sons would rule for at least the next four generations in Samaria. It was what Jehu did *after* the slaughter of the house of Ahab that displeased God and changed Jehu's reputation and fortunes.

When all Jehu's killing — ultimately at the instruction of Elisha — had been finished, he settled down and became a regent who earned the infamous characterization of not turning away from the "sins of Jeroboam," the earliest of the rebels against the united kingdom. Jeroboam had made such a name for himself as evil, that most wicked kings after him were said to have followed in his footsteps. He built golden calves and had the northern tribes worship them instead of going to Jerusalem.

Jehu revived the worship of Jeroboam's golden calves (2 Kings 10:29). Apparently this idolatry wiped out the blessing of God on his obedience in being the executioner of the house of Ahab. In using his grand promotion to king ultimately to champion the worship of idols he prostituted the entire nation, canceling the purpose of removing the house of Ahab. Now, the "blood of Jezreel" became not the symbol of Jehu's obedience to God, but instead the emblem of his violent accession to the throne of Israel where he proceeded to lead the nation further into wickedness.

In naming his first child Jezreel, Hosea was told it was because God was going to punish the house of Jehu for the massacre, and in so doing was going to bring Israel's dynasty to a close. Jehu would have his own Jezreel.

6 **And she conceived again, and bare a daughter. And God said unto him, Call her name Loruhamah: for I will no more have mercy upon the house of Israel; but I will utterly take them away.**

The second child was a daughter, **Lo-Ruhamah,** "not pitied," or "not shown compassion." One can think of any number of unfortunate surnames in the English world, many of which had no negative associations when first chosen. But the last name "Loveless" also comes to mind, as a close parallel to the name Hosea had to give his daughter. The firstborn boy's name gave the overview of judgment. The second child pictured the first stage of judgment: Hosea's generation would not be spared the punishment. The enormity of the nation's sin earned a corresponding measure of wrath.

It would be possible to argue that God's demand that these children bear these names is more evidence for interpreting "children of harlotry" as the "offspring of adulterous liaisons." The reasoning would be that the names God ordered for them would have been cruel had they been Hosea's children instead of the progeny of some nameless adulterer Gomer lay with. Would God treat innocent children this way? The flaw in this reasoning is that *all* children are innocent of the sins of their parents, adulterous or not.

It is also possible that while the names were recorded as given, each may have been called by some nickname on a regular basis.

But though there was punishment planned, the long term purpose was redemption. If God didn't care about Israel, he simply would have discarded her. The fact is that he cared enough to discipline her and that he intended to save her:

7   **But I will have mercy upon the house of Judah, and will save them by the LORD their God, and will not save them by bow, nor by sword, nor by battle, by horses, nor by horsemen.**

The northern kingdom, Israel, would come to an end, as would the south, in their defeat by Assyria. The difference was that the northern kingdom would never rise again, while the southern would—not as a kingdom. Some of its refugees would be part of the southern peoples in the repopulation of the areas the two kingdoms had inhabited. The annihilation of the northern but the salvation of the southern kingdom said that any hope the people of Israel — the northern kingdom — had of recovery must be vested in the south, whose kings were in the line of David. But even there, the salvation of the southern kingdom would not come by military might—**bow, sword, battle, horses,** and **horsemen.**

Like the well-known verse, "Not by might, nor by power, but by my Spirit, saith the LORD" (Zechariah 4:6), this verse emphasizes that when

God saved, it would not be by the attempt of Israel or Judah to save herself. It would instead be through a sovereign act that would be inexplicable apart from the intervention of the Almighty.

Historically, the punishment of Israel was to come through its overthrow by a foreign power, a period of captivity to follow. No alliance they sought, with Egypt, Judah, or anybody else, was to keep them from being captured. And when, after more than seventy years, they were freed to return to their land, it would not be because of their internal revolt, or because of some marauding power defeating their captors, but instead because of the sovereign act of God in changing the hearts of despots.

Accordingly, the message includes the promise of renewal after the prophecy of judgment:

8 **Now when she had weaned Loruhamah, she conceived, and bare a son.**

9 **Then said God, Call his name Loammi: for ye are not my people, and I will not be your God.**

The third child was a son, named **Lo-Ammi** — "not my people." It was the antithesis of the covenant formula (Exodus 6:7, Deuteronomy 26:17, Jeremiah 31:33). Expressed in terms of Hosea's marriage, God was declaring the severe state of disruption between the covenant people and himself.

Through Hosea's rocky home life and his pointing to his own life as he preached, Israel was to hear the message that it was being grossly unfaithful to God, and that it would be judged severely for its behavior.

10 **Yet the number of the children of Israel shall be as the sand of the sea, which cannot be measured nor numbered...**

The emphasis on this little word **Yet**—incorporated in the word *wᵊhayah*, cannot be understated. It acts as a fulcrum on which the sovereign plan of God shifts from judgment to redemption, the hinge on which the disposition of God turns from wrath to blessing.

The amazing part about this book, with all its blunt honesty in rebuke of the sins of Israel, is its repetition of the promise made to Abraham, that his descendants would be like **the sand of the sea.** It may be beyond their lifetimes, but their people would return. In that day, God would hold them dear.

…and it shall come to pass, that in the place where it was said unto them, Ye are not my people, there it shall be said unto them, Ye are the sons of the living God.

"[S]ons of the living God" is opposite of "not my people," but it shifts to different terminology. Where now they are not "the people" of God—a collective term—eventually they will be "the sons of God"—an individual term. This emphasis on the individual relationship may give us a clue that God is revealing to Hosea a future that lies beyond a mere recovery of a homeland. Possibly this points to the time of spiritual redemption brought by the long promised Messiah.

11 **Then shall the children of Judah and the children of Israel be gathered together, and appoint themselves one head, and they shall come up out of the land: for great shall be the day of Jezreel.**

Hosea's vision is of the reunification of the southern and northern kingdoms, which would take place in an interesting way following seventy years of captivity. The primacy of Judah and Benjamin would be evident at that point, the northern tribes represented in the returning peoples in small numbers. The "one head" *(ehad ros)* signified the national unification, and initially their governor was Ezra. However, the ultimate significance of the verse looks far beyond the second-temple period, to a day in which a divinely appointed Messiah would rule all God's people.

Chapter 2

The next chapter of Hosea begins with an interesting amalgam of lament and accusation. It is the harsh word of rebuke one speaks to a beloved who has abandoned the faithfulness that was pledged and has broken the spiritual bond that united them. Israel used to be the wife of the LORD, but no longer.

The second chapter as divided in the Hebrew during the mid fifteenth century A.D. began with a verse that seems to many interpreters to belong with chapter 1 instead of chapter 2. Which body of verses it belongs with determines the basic interpretation of it.

1   **Say ye unto your brethren, Ammi; and to your sisters, Ruhamah.**
2   **Plead with your mother, plead; for she is not my wife, neither am I her husband...**

There really is no consensus as to whether the verse attaches to the previous words or the following ones. Many commentaries offer both views for consideration without commitment.

The New Living Translation assumes the connection is with chapter 1, adding a transition phrase and changing the tense of the verb: "In that day you *will* call your brothers Ammi—'my people' (etc.) (emphasis ours). The assumption may go too far in amending the text.

Several translators who connect the verse with chapter 1 add "So" to the beginning as a connector to chapter 2 (CEV, GWT, ISV).

The Coverdale Bible (1535) and the Bishops' Bible (1568) both say, "Tell your brethren that they are my people, and your sisterne, that they haue obtayned mercy" (spelling, Bishops'), taking the verse as capping off the thought of chapter 1.

The GNT has, "My children, plead with your mother," tying together vv1-2 as if v1 has a comma after it instead of a period, as most other translations employ. Since the Hebrew had no punctuation, it's the translators' best guess.

We find that 2:1 is not a complete sentence; it is an address to the few, still-faithful people of Israel, begging them in 2:2 to warn their neighbors and countrymen about their sin. Thus, **Ammi** and **Ruhamma** in v1 are *appositives* of the dual subjects **brothers** and **sisters.** The two verses would then read:

> Say to your brothers (my people) and to your sisters (my beloved), "Please plead with your mother!"

While Hosea's family was the ongoing parable of the nation's life, 2:1 is clearly not addressed to them (his only girl would not have been called "sisters"); instead, it was spoken to some persons in the nation. During Elijah's ministry, when he claimed before the Lord that "I, even I only, am left," God revealed, "I have left me seven thousand in Israel, all the knees which have not bowed unto Baal" (1 Kings 19:14,18). So here, though the character of the northern kingdom was wretched and perverse, rife with idolatry, there were some, the salt of whose lives had to that moment preserved the nation, who could be reached with a plea. In a kind of envisionment of the nation's future reclamation by God, Hosea's urgent request is to a small group of people scattered around the country who had not fallen prey to the nation's rampant sins.

Chapter 1 is really an overview of the whole plan of God, to judge Israel and Judah, to punish them by cutting them off and dispersing them, then to reunite them in an act of redemption and salvation, making them more the people of God than they ever were.

Chapter two begins a poetic version of the warning and prophecy delivered by Hosea to Israel. As one of them, he speaks of them as family, and invites them to speak to one another of their common need to repent.

As sometimes husbands and wives engage their children in attempts to communicate with each other, so Hosea calls to the adulterous wife through the pleadings of the children: **Plead with your mother.** Perhaps he did so in actuality in his own family—the children may have known exactly where Gomer was, but not Hosea—but more importantly, he is pleading with spiritually aware persons in Israel to speak out to their country, their countrymen, their king, anybody who will listen. As students refer to the schools that graduated them as "alma mater" —nourishing mother— so Hosea pleads with the people of Israel to act like children of their mother country, in convincing her to return to the Lord. God instructs Hosea to stir other concerned Israelites to raise the public consciousness about the desperate need of repentance. It would be similar to modern political activists urging people to write their congressmen and senators, attend rallies and make noise in public in any way possible.

The KJV's "**Plead**" is followed by numerous other translators in this word choice, but more modern versions say "Contend" or "Rebuke," or even "Bring charges." Interestingly, the New Living Translation, which connected 2:1 with chapter 1 ("In that day you will call your brothers Ammi") adds a transition phrase to 2:2, rendering it, "But now bring charges against Israel…" The NLT sees 2:1 as looking far into the future, and 2:2 as calling the reader-listener's attention back to the present, and to the difficulty and danger of the circumstances.

… let her therefore put away her whoredoms out of her sight, and her adulteries from between her breasts.

Almost all modern versions read the Hebrew "sight" *(mippaneh)* as "face," as it is rendered multiple other places in the OT. Thus the NIV's "remove the adulterous look from her face." This accords better with the context than the KJV's rendering.

If the **look** on the face—the sultry, 'come-hither' look, or more probably the make-up that identified a prostitute—is obvious enough, the **adulteries from between her breasts** is not as self-evident. Some think it is a description of the position of a lover reclining on her body. Others hold it refers to a necklace with a pendant or amulet symbolizing a Baal. That women of Israel, or anyone for that matter, would wear these symbols that declared their loyalty to, or love of, some other supposed deity was an affront to God, and one that he did not take lightly.

Taking the two phrases referencing the face and breasts to refer to the adulteress's invitation and then a physical description of the ensuing encounter, the GNT renders this part of the verse, "Plead with her to stop her adultery and prostitution." That phrasing certainly is a practical restatement, but it misses the poetry—or deliberately eliminates it—from the original author's language.

The entire chapter is poetry, as we have noted. In it Hosea intricately entwines a description and rebuke of his wife and her unfaithfulness with an account and accusation of Israel's idolatry and its attendant sins. It is difficult, to the point of being impossible, to separate the two, to know at some point whether Hosea is speaking of Gomer or the northern kingdom in its entirety. This nearly seamless interweaving is intentional and is masterfully crafted.

As a result, in interpreting the chapter and much of the rest of the book, the reader is justified in mingling the symbol with its significance, letting the poetic imagery communicate the thought without insisting on robbing the language of its purely emotional impact.

3   **Lest I strip her naked, and set her as in the day that she was born, and make her as a wilderness...**

While prostitutes had no shame in being naked with their clients, to be thrust naked into public view was quite another thing.

Some of human beings' worst nightmares are of finding themselves somewhere in public wearing little to no clothing. It's a universal expression of waking fears of other things. However, when Hosea wrote, "**Lest I strip her naked,**" what made this image of judgment so vivid for the Israelites was that in surrounding cultures there was a history of practice regarding divorce, in which the husband would pronounce the divorce, then strip his wife and put her outside the house. The listener who translated that knowledge of domestic divorce into an issue of national rebuke by God had some sense of what he intended to do to Israel.

The text made the judgment explicit: **set her as in the day she was born.** The Hebrew has *wəhissagtiha,* "and expose her." The stripping was for the purpose of exposure to the view of others. In the following phrase, **"and make her as a wilderness,"** some versions have "desert." The word is *kammidbar,* which will appear again in 2:14. The wilderness of the general area of Israel is not like the Sahara, with nothing but sand for hundreds of miles. It is, however, relatively dry and barren, supporting only the hardiest of life. It is somewhat ironical and greatly illustrative that in the region of Judah and Israel places of lush and productive beauty are often surprisingly close to—even contiguous with—areas of barrenness and hardship. This is a metaphor of life, where wrong directions can eventuate in wilderness wanderings in short order.

...and set her like a dry land...

Again, "set" is *wəsattiha,* to make or render. What she, the nation, will become will be God's doing, not the accidental result of her own missteps.

...and slay her with thirst...

This judgment, symbolized in nakedness, barrenness and thirst, speaks of (1) humiliation, (2) shame, and (3) deprivation. These qualities are typical of all kinds of situations God may use to bring nations, and individuals, under discipline for their sin.

But it isn't for simple satisfaction of anger that God brings such things to pass. It is instead to demonstrate that he is the one who clothes us with righteousness, provides for our needs, covers our sin, and removes our shame. Without him, there is the absence of all that is good.

4   **And I will not have mercy upon her children; for they be the children of whoredoms.**

5   **For their mother hath played the harlot: she that conceived them hath done shamefully...**

We hold that chapter 1 makes sufficiently clear that Hosea's children were not fathered by other men. If we are correct, **conceived** *(howratam)* would be a metaphor for the culture's creation of more and more spiritually adulterous people. The idea is that simply because new generations that arise are not guilty of their parents' sins does not mean they will be exempt from the national judgment. They are purveyors of their own sins, of course, but they are also the inheritors of a system of values and morals that they have not actively rejected.

What follows then is a list of charges against Israel, and the corresponding divine discipline, all dressed in the language of the marital relationship.

...she said, I will go after my lovers, that give me my bread and my water, my wool and my flax, mine oil and my drink...

The Baals did not at all provide these things, due to the fact that they were non-existent "beings." Even if we understand that fallen spiritual beings inhabited the nations around Israel and were thought to be present in the idols those peoples worshiped, these spiritual beings did not themselves possess the powers that only Yahweh possessed—to bless with harvest or punish with famine. This is precisely the point Hosea was making, and the deprivation Israel would experience under judgment would prove this point. Fertility was not to be found in a phantasm.

The idea of fertility worship was essentially that earth was considered to be female, Baal to be a male, and rain therefore to be sperm of sorts. Fertility rites were engaged in so as to convince Baal on a constant basis to "deposit" his blessings on the earth and keep her fertile. The sexual concepts of their gods help to explain the extremely sensual conduct of Israelite worship, adopted from pagan cultures.

6   Therefore, behold, I will hedge up thy way with thorns, and make
    a wall, that she shall not find her paths.
7   And she shall follow after her lovers, but she shall not overtake
    them; and she shall seek them, but shall not find them: then shall
    she say, I will go and return to my first husband; for then was it
    better with me than now.

The divine purpose is to withdraw from Israel what Jesus later
would describe as God's general grace in making his 'sun to rise on the
evil and on the good, and his rain to fall on the just and on the unjust'
(Matthew 5:45). In the ensuing famine and general misery, perhaps
Israel would turn back to the Lord.

The verb **hedge up** *(sak)* does not appear to represent any actual
parallel in human activity in Hosea's immediate family, though
throughout history some suspicious and jealous husbands have been
known to prohibit their wives' leaving the house. Again, the symbolic
view of Hosea's family is far more likely.

In saying that God would **make a wall, that she shall not find her
paths,** this language aptly describes mazes, in ancient times called
labyrinths. Coins have been found from about 400 B.C. depicting
mazes. Although the garden mazes of the 18th century A.D. were
designed for entertainment, early labyrinths had the purpose of
representing a spiritual journey. They offered the opportunity for
contemplation and meditation. However, they could also induce panic.

The experience of Israel, whose real-life national situation was about
to be beset with international danger, was no game. God promised to
put his people in a maze of frustration, confusion, difficulty, failure, and
emptiness, in order to convince them that they needed the living Lord,
not a worthless Baal.

Objective analysis of idol worship easily discredits it on several
grounds, but the historical record of Israel's attraction to idolatry from

the time of their beginnings through the start of their captivity raises the pressing question of what so drew them to it repeatedly, against all warnings. From biblical and other sources describing Baal worship among the ancients, it is apparent that the characteristics of Baal making him attractive as a deity were that he was: (1) visible; (2) indulgent; (3) tolerant; and (4) flexible.

...she shall seek them, but shall not find them...

Again, this is not Gomer but the people of Israel, whom God said at some point would become disillusioned with the false gods she has been pursuing, when those deities failed to save their worshipers from national crises.

It is equally God's intention to convince his people down through the ages to conclude that the cultural gods they run after are worthless, when these things they value more than the Lord are unable to help them get through the tough things that life brings about. Non-existent gods cannot give wisdom for decisions, strength for struggles, or hope for hours of suffering and death. If reason and sensibility won't cause people to look up, perhaps being laid flat on their backs will.

...my first husband...

The Hebrew is *isi harisown.* "First" has the expected meaning, along with a little shade of "foremost." There is also a deliberate intermingling of the symbol—Hosea—with the one symbolized—the Lord God.

...for then was it better with me than now.

This is precisely the reaction God wants. Note the similarity of the reasoning, i.e. "better off," to the thinking of the prodigal son in Jesus' parable: "How many hired servants of my father's have bread enough and to spare, and I perish with hunger!" (Luke 15:17). Depriving Israel of the abundance they credit Baal with giving them is meant to result in their remembering the Lord.

8   For she did not know that I gave her corn, and wine, and oil, and multiplied her silver and gold, which they prepared for Baal.

Israel's sin was more than simply neglecting to thank God for her material blessings; it was in actually using them in the worship of another god. This perversion of his blessings sparked God's wrath.

Even if people have no crass, primitive images before which to bow and make offerings, they have the invisible, sophisticated idols of money, philosophies, or themselves, on which they lavish their means and the things of this world. Any talent used to exploit people to enrich self is a perversion of something God gave to be used for his glory.

9   Therefore will I return, and take away my corn in the time thereof...

In other words, in its season, or when it ripens. KJV **corn** is not maze but grain, most likely wheat or another bread grain. This may have been a prediction of unexpected crop failures. Every farmer knows that either too little rain or rain at the *wrong* time ruins wheat. Other blight may also have been in the mind of the divine judge.

...and my wine in the season thereof...

In addition to too little rain, a host of fungal, viral or bacteriological diseases will ruin a grape harvest and thus the production of new wine. Most of these diseases still have no cure.

...and will recover my wool and my flax given to cover her nakedness.

Recover is take back or take away. Again, the method was likely to be something that the godless in heart could be angry at or simply confused about, but those with a word from the Lord might realize their predicament was his divine hand, trying to convince them to return to him.

10 And now will I discover her lewdness in the sight of her lovers...

The NLT, GNT and CEV have "strip her naked" for **discover her lewdness**, and the CSB has "expose her shame." While nakedness itself, out of context, is not shameful, in the context of exposing adultery it is likely to be dramatically felt so by the one stripped. The Hebrew *nablutah* is used only here in the OT, with several related forms of the word appearing elsewhere translated as "corpse." In Eden, the human body, unclothed as were all the creatures in the earth, was the magnificent natural creation of God, which to Adam and Eve was beautiful to each other. Sin brought them a sense of shame in being naked without privacy. In the later practice of exposure as punishment for sexual sin, what was innocent between married partners became lewd when poisoned by what people did with God's beautiful gift.

...and none shall deliver her out of mine hand.

No rescue will take place until God has done what he plans to do. "It is a fearful thing to fall into the hands of the living God!" (Hebrews 10:31).

11 I will also cause all her mirth to cease, her feast days, her new moons, and her sabbaths, and all her solemn feasts.

It is important to realize that Israel was attempting to incorporate the worship of Baal and other gods into her observance of the feasts of the worship of the Lord. It may confuse the reader to wonder how Israelites could manage the mental—to say nothing of the spiritual —gymnastics it should have taken to justify this kind of syncretism, given the exclusivity at the core of the worship of Yahweh. But Israel had virtually gutted the worship of the Lord in favor of a hollow shell of observances—which were relatively meaningless in the absence of the heart of the faith. Nevertheless, they continued to observe some or many of those feasts and generate the external celebration, just as they learned the festivities of Baal worship. But God was going to take all sense of joy out of Israel's rituals, perhaps replacing it with a growing unease, a sense of the doom that was coming.

12 And I will destroy her vines and her fig trees, whereof she hath said, These are my rewards that my lovers have given me...

"Rewards" is *etnah*, rendered variously as "pay," "gifts," or "wages" in modern translations. Again, the imagery of Gomer and the larger population are mingled. For a society to forget God and credit their own ingenuity and hard work for their abundance is one thing, but for that culture to ascribe their national success to a pagan god would be a vile perversion.

...and I will make them a forest, and the beasts of the field shall eat them.

The picture is of crops long failed and undergrowth overtaking cultivated areas.

13 And I will visit upon her the days of Baalim...

Literally, "I will punish her for the days of the Baals."

...wherein she burned incense to them...

The adulterous woman symbolized by the true-to-life parable in Hosea's own life tries redoubling her worship of Baal, burning incense to the various iterations of his image, in her appeal to this national god. Economic losses, loss of integrity, loss of joy, national depression and malaise, have descended on the nation, in this visual prophecy of Hosea's. But for all her appeal to Baal, Israel will go downhill constantly, until she realizes why it's all happening.

One could easily see the reverberations of such epochs of judgment down through the centuries. A country where the worship of God once flourished experiences: economic troubles; the mysterious appearance of diseases befalling almost exclusively those engaged in sexual and other sins; international loss of prestige; internal dissension; violence; crime; and other things. The country's response: raise taxes to try to buy themselves out of economic malaise; promote "safe" ways to sin to avoid disease; seek world government to counteract international crises; and restructure education to impose social engineering. Where is the appeal to God?

Humanity lives in what might be called a spiritual ecosystem, all parts functioning together correctly only if the underlying assumptions, premises and foundations are properly intact. That happens only when the LORD is God.

...she decked herself with her earrings and her jewels, and she went after her lovers, and forgat me, saith the LORD.

Jewelry and earrings have long been ways women have attempted to make themselves more alluring. As devices of worship, they attest to the fact that the concept of Baal was sexual in nature.

Further, Israel's pursuit of Baal was entirely within their knowledge of its abhorrence to God. When people thumb their noses at God, deliberately rejecting his way in order to do what they please, they have reached the height of sin's obstinacy and perverseness.

Israel's sin was great; but where sin abounds, amazingly grace abounds all the more (Romans 5:20). God wasn't finished with his first wife yet. He intended to win her hand—again:

14 Therefore, behold, I will allure her...

It isn't always the case that the understood pronoun associated with a verb form is expressed, and when it is, it indicates emphasis. Here, "I" is a separate word in the Hebrew, creating that emphasis. The only reasonable purpose for this stress is to create contrast between "I," the LORD and the implied competing suitors, Baal or another god being worshiped in Israel. The comparison is dual: The Lord wooed Israel where Baal, who didn't exist, couldn't and didn't woo them; and the

Lord would pursue Israel whereas Israel had pursued Baal.

…and bring her into the wilderness…

The word **wilderness** appears here again. In the previous instance, God was preparing to turn Israel herself into a wilderness; here, he brings her into the wilderness with allurement. The function of the wilderness is not the same, however. Where the previous focus was on the barrenness that would characterize her life under judgment, here the focus is on the privacy of the place. The scene is set for the Lord to reveal his grace to her.

Consequently, **wilderness** indicates a retreat, and a separation from the environment in which Israel has been unfaithful. A key strategy for winning them—or us—back to God, is alienation from the support systems of wrongdoing, and an environment in which total dependence on God may be learned. This was what the desert, or wilderness, before entrance into Canaan taught Israel.

Our own wildernesses may be physical, but more likely will be situational, i.e., circumstances in which we lose the false foundations of security and have no one but God to go to. For us, it may take losing jobs, losing loved ones, going bankrupt, being faced with tragedy or terror, to open our eyes. The wise person will not let things progress so far before he returns from the "far country."

…and speak comfortably unto her.

"Comfortably" *(libbah)* is the same root word as in Isaiah 40:2, "Speak ye comfortably *(leb)* to Jerusalem." Most modern versions have "tenderly." The stark contrast between the mood of this verse and that of 3-13 underscores the ability of God to finish his discipline and hold out his arms in invitation without any residue of anger.

This is a fascinating turn of events. God is angry because Israel has succumbed to the advances of other religions. His first response—not a knee jerk reaction but nevertheless the priority that must be observed—is to punish her appropriately to teach her a lesson and turn her around. But now he says he is going to turn on some allurement of his own. Hosea uses the same concept of seduction, if we may say so respectfully, to describe God's intention to win back Israel. This is what any determined man will do if the object of his affections shows interest in other men.

This is instructive, because it shows that God doesn't simply become irritated with his people and dispense with them, but instead re-intensifies his efforts to cause them to fall in love with him again.

An interpretive question raised by v14 is whether the wilderness into which God will entreat Israel is actually her captivity in Assyria. Historically, there was no period of relief that took place between Hosea's time and the fall of Israel to Samaria in 722 B.C. It seems the likeliest interpretation to see the upcoming years in captivity as being indicated, though to begin with the experience would hardly seem like a romantic retreat.

However, what was startling about the captivity was the success the Jewish people experienced there and the eventual favor they obtained in the eyes of their rulers. Where they were forcibly removed from their home to begin with, they were favorably allowed to return to that home later, and with the blessing of their captors.

15 And I will give her her vineyards from thence, and the valley of Achor for a door of hope...

"From thence," or "from there," is treated in many modern versions as meaning "give back" or "return." This is the implication, though many translators think "there" probably refers to the place of captivity, and so they leave the phrase alone and render it strictly. Interestingly, the Douay-Rheims Bible says, "vinedressers out of the same place," suggesting clearly that the place of captivity is meant, as God turns the place of discipline into a place of fruitfulness.

Achor means "trouble." Israel passed through the Valley of Achor on the way up to the promised land. It was named Achor for Achan, whose sin and punishment taught Israel the importance of faithfulness to God's commands.

Sometimes trouble doesn't turn people *to* God, but *away* from him; but this is the choice of man, not the fault of God.

...and she shall sing there, as in the days of her youth, and as in the day when she came up out of the land of Egypt.

While "the day when she came up out of the land of Egypt" brings to mind the exodus *from* a place of slavery, Hosea's prophesied singing of Israel takes place "there," i.e. in the place of her upcoming captivity, or at the very least when she begins to return—some seventy years hence—to her homeland. She will have been properly chastised, redirected, revived spiritually, and focused on coming back to the previously promised land to serve the Lord faithfully.

But Hosea, reading the heart of the Lord in the word he hears from him, anticipates an eventual fundamental difference in the relationship of God's people to him:

16 **And it shall be at that day, saith the LORD, that thou shalt call me Ishi; and shalt call me no more Baali.**

The notable thing about this prediction is the change of names, which in English versions are simple transliterations of the Hebrew. *Ishi,* is "husband," the name for a man in a relationship of love and devotion. *Ba'li* is "master," the name of one who demands slavish subservience. It is no accident that the name of the chief "master" of the idolatrous region is simply Baal.

17 **For I will take away the names of Baalim out of her mouth...**

In a reading of Israel's history from the time of the beginning of the divided kingdom to the day of their being conquered, what is most striking is how quickly and easily Israel turned away from the Lord and followed the idol worship of the peoples they had failed to displace entirely during the conquest described in Joshua. Israel's fundamental fickleness in spiritual things proved first the shallowness of the belief and worship of most of the nation, and second the wisdom in God's having commanded them to drive out all the inhabitants of Canaan and the other regions they conquered. The peoples they left, some of whom they simply could not dislodge and others who became their servants, retained their pagan worship, and its influence eventually captivated Israelite minds.

What is implied directly by God's "taking away" the very names of the Baals is a change of heart in which the Israelites who return to their land are enabled to devote themselves to the Lord.

18 **And in that day will I make a covenant for them with the beasts of the field, and with the fowls of heaven, and with the creeping things of the ground...**

In Genesis 2:19 God created the beasts of the field and the fowls of the air, and in Eden there was harmony and untainted goodness. Much happened since that day, in the human race as well as in the broader creation. Yet the prophecy of what ultimately lies in store for God's people is a return to the bliss and blessing of Eden.

...and I will break the bow and the sword and the battle out of the earth, and will make them to lie down safely.

A "covenant" *(bərit)* with the animal kingdom speaks of the return of creation to its original state.

Breaking the bow, sword and battle have the same prophetic foreshadowing of final peace as Isaiah 2:4 and Micah 4:3, where God's people "will beat their swords into plowshares and their spears into pruning hooks."

The resulting force of v18 is therefore one of eschatological significance. In what is commonly referred to as prophetic foreshortening, the message of Hosea leaps from the return and revival expected a few years hence to the one hoped for ultimately, after which there will be no more fears of captivity, no more threat of war, no competing worship of idols, and indeed no more sin.

19 And I will betroth thee unto me for ever...

Betrothal, in Jewish culture, was a little more than modern engagement. It was a step in the bringing together of two people, culminating in marriage. "Betroth" here, *(waerastik),* is inclusive of its goal of marriage, since betrothal set in motion the process that was almost never interrupted.

...yea, I will betroth thee unto me in righteousness, and in judgment, and in lovingkindness, and in mercies.

The ISV adds some words to fill out the thought: "in a way that is righteous, in a manner that is just, by a love that is gracious, and by a motive that is mercy." While the added words are not in the text, they probably capture the thought.

Judgment is better "justice," and **mercies** is probably more contemporarily accurate as "compassion." The point is that Israel is not being brought like a wife into the tent of a suitor who plans for her a life of subservience out of a "relationship" of distance. The Lord fully intends for Israel to be joined to him in a close relationship of love, characterized by all his perfect qualities, which will overshadow and eventually come to be reflected in her.

Further:

20 I will even betroth thee unto me in faithfulness: and thou shalt know the LORD.

The GNT has, "I will keep my promise and make you mine," taking "faithfulness" as what leads God to be united with Israel (so also the NLT). Most other versions give no hint as to whether their translators thought the faithfulness *(be'emunah)* was the reason for the betrothal or the resulting conduct of God. Clearly, however, it is both, and it could not be otherwise: "If we believe not, yet he abideth faithful: he cannot deny himself" (2 Timothy 2:13).

The language of marriage continues through the perhaps surprising but nevertheless consistent image of Israel's "knowing" the LORD, a common euphemism in the OT for sexual relations when applied to human unions.

There is no suggestion in this language of the kind of crass atmosphere of sexuality that was present in the worship of the Baals. Nowhere before and nowhere after in scripture is any hint given that the proper worship of God is to involve temple prostitution or sexual acts of any kind. These were the perversions of idol worship, the appeals perhaps of fallen spiritual entities inspiring that worship to provide for them the atmosphere they craved, in the sensuality that embodied humanity had. By the most holy contrast, in the case of God and Israel, their unity was to be an intimacy of spiritual love and possession, as they learned to worship him "in spirit and in truth" (John 4:24).

There is also an echo of the thought in Jeremiah 31:34: "And they shall teach no more every man his neighbour, and every man his brother, saying, Know the LORD: for they shall all know me, from the least of them unto the greatest of them, saith the LORD."

Both the short view of the prophet and the eschatological view envision a future with a happy ending. It was, as it still is, the need of humanity to be able to rest their hopes on the promise of better things to come.

In further describing the far-off future of Israel, Hosea writes the word of God that came to his heart about where, not just Israel's history, but also heilsgeschichte—holy history—is headed. When the prophets skipped from what could be more easily envisioned a few generations away to what was more difficult to imagine an unknown epoch away, they were not entirely without awareness of the missing historical material in their descriptions. Hebrews 11:39-40 states that the ancients were commended for their faith, but that "they without us should not be made perfect." The author of Hebrews implies that the Old Testament people who lived by faith knew very well something more perfect was coming, something only prefigured by their own experience of blessing, renewal, and national deliverance. One cannot read Hosea and not sense his awareness of eschatological hopes. The thought in 2:14-20 continues in 2:21-23:

21 And it shall come to pass in that day, I will hear, saith the LORD, I will hear the heavens, and they shall hear the earth...

Hosea depicts a sort of cosmic conversation between the heavens and the earth, in which the earth cries out its need for rain, and the heavens hear and report to God, asking for orders. This is the divinely created ecosystem. God the sovereign permits rain; rain comes down because the earth needs it; the earth provides nutrients because grain needs them; grain grows because Jezreel, the valley, and the people therein, need it; and Israel, planted in the valley by God, is nourished by it all. God understands the biosphere: he made it. And though it operates according to the built-in mechanics of molecular, chemical, and physical properties, God is still ultimately in charge. Blessing, or judgment, are in his hands.

22 And the earth shall hear the corn, and the wine, and the oil; and they shall hear Jezreel.

When the heavens have received their orders and have rained, the earth hears the petitions of the crops and grows them.

The name "Jezreel" comes from two roots meaning "to sow" and "Almighty." When spoken of earlier in the naming of Hosea's first child, the word was mostly an allusion to the place Jezreel, where Jehu had slaughtered so many royals. But once the name was given to

Hosea's son, its significance lingered in the mind as an implicit prophecy. First, it had the meaning of sowing as scattering, and the idea was negative. But here, where God makes "Jezreel" part of the ecosystem equation, it is actually a name for Israel that depicts her being planted in the world by that scattering, the manner of sowing the seed:

23 And I will sow her unto me in the earth...

Many translators render *ba'ares* as "land," but as the KJV, NKJV and several others indicate by their word choice, the land is really the entire "earth." This is a prophecy of God's people—including all the eventual people of biblical faith—being divine seed sown throughout God's world, there to grow until the final harvest.

...and I will have mercy upon her that had not obtained mercy; and I will say to them which were not my people, Thou art my people; and they shall say, Thou art my God.

At the culmination of the kingdom of God, Hosea envisions a great inclusion of those who previously had been labeled as "not obtaining mercy" and "not my people," in an event that changes their relationship to God and their eternal destiny. For then, they will be the recipients of mercy and they will be God's people again. And their response to God's mercy and inclusion will be their joyful declaration: You are my God! (*elohay*).

This verse shares the dual fulfillment expected since v14. The joy of the Israelites' return to their land in 538 B.C. and following was mitigated by the fact that they were ruled by others. But the ultimate return envisioned is a spiritual return, irrespective of geographical location. Those whom God has sown (*uzəratiha*) will continue to propagate where planted throughout the earth until they are brought back into the kingdom of those who believe the whole word of God, receiving mercy for salvation and full inclusion into God's family.

Chapter 3

Beginning with chapter 3, Hosea delivers with additional details God's forecast of the distant future, including some revealing words about a time just past in history.

1　**Then said the LORD unto me, Go yet, love a woman beloved of her friend, yet an adulteress, according to the love of the LORD toward the children of Israel, who look to other gods, and love flagons of wine.**

Textual problems make unclear just who this "woman" is. Some ancient sources interpret her as someone other than Gomer, presuming Gomer to have been divorced by Hosea. But there is nothing else in the context of the book to support this view.

Another—and a major—textual problem is how to render "friend" *(rea),* for the woman is beloved of this friend. There is great division in modern translations. The NIV, ESV and CSB all say she is loved by "another man," who is implicitly not Hosea. Some other versions have "another," or "a lover," or otherwise imply someone other than Hosea. The NKJV even departs from the KJV in saying, somewhat cryptically, "loved by a lover." However, the NASB resolutely says, "who is loved by her husband," and the Amplified Bible concurs with, "beloved by her husband." A few translations waffle on the matter with word choices that could be interpreted either way.

Those translators who clearly come down on the side of this "other person" being a man other than Hosea regularly render *um ʾna'apet* as "and is an adulteress" or something similar. Those who take *rea* to be a reference to Hosea render *um ʾna'apet* "*yet* is an adulteress," drawing the contrast between the husband the woman has and the lover she has nevertheless taken.

We take the "woman" to be Gomer, and the "friend" to be Hosea. Nothing else in the book suggests that Hosea started over again, wooing a second wife. In fact, the entire metaphor depends on the imagery of the pursuit of *one,* through thick and thin.

The two sins of Israel, the national adulterous woman, that are pointed out are looking to "other gods," and loving "flagons of wine." The worship of "other gods" notoriously involved sexual activity of all kinds. And excessive drinking of wine and other strong drink was the norm both in the context of worship and elsewhere. As to free sex as common entertainment and rampant consumption of alcoholic beverages, the relevance of such a description to the present day is striking.

2   So I bought her to me for fifteen pieces of silver, and for an homer of barley, and an half homer of barley:

What necessitated Gomer's being bought was, as most interpreters agree, some sort of indenture to a paramour who basically stole her for his own, or to a Baal cult as a prostitute. The cults may have acted in a way similar to sex trafficking in the modern day. We are not given the details. However, the price was not by any means exorbitant. She wasn't worth much to those who used her and abused her. There were more where she came from.

3   And I said unto her, Thou shalt abide for me many days; thou shalt not play the harlot, and thou shalt not be for another man: so will I also be for thee.

It was Hosea's plan for Gomer to stay with him for "many days." The Vulgate's translation takes this to mean "wait for me many days," meaning a period of separation sexually even though she would be in the household. Whether or not this is accurate, having retrieved her from her virtual slavery, Hosea did apparently restrict her to the household. There might have been no other way for him to prohibit her clandestine involvement with yet another lover, as a prostitute or not.

The interpretive question for this verse is what is meant by the last words, *wǝgam ani elayik,* literally "so too I (will be) toward you." Even in light of Gomer's being ordered not to "play the harlot," Hosea cannot be saying he won't be unfaithful to her either, because that much is a given. Instead, he appears to be informing her that while she is being restricted to the home so as to keep her out of temptation, he also will restrict his sexual relationship with regard to her—abstinence. Perhaps the sexual component for her was an addiction, which needed breaking.

So then, Hosea bought his wife out of prostitution, put her under discipline in his house, kept her from returning to prostitution, and denied her sexual union even with him. This distance in sexual intimacy shows that his concentration was on the more substantial and sacrificial nature of his love for her, and that until she showed the fruits of repentance and change, the closest fellowship was not even possible.

4 For the children of Israel shall abide many days without a king, and without a prince, and without a sacrifice, and without an image, and without an ephod, and without teraphim:

Now the "many days" of v3 are applied to Israel the nation. Obviously Hosea saw the soon-coming captivity, and it goes without saying that Israel would be without king, prince, or sacrifice. These first three are deprivations of things legitimately belonging to Israel's self-governance and worship. The remaining three terms can then be taken as things that probably related to illegitimate, proscribed worship: images, ephods and teraphim. While **ephod**s were used in the worship of the LORD, similar garments existed in Baal worship. And the **image**s and **teraphim** (household gods) were also elements in foreign religions. The verse suggests that Israel would be deprived of her own worship but also that she would be distanced from the idolatries that had continually allured her over the centuries.

The ultimate fulfillment of this prophecy would extend a *long time* into the future, after the return to Israel but also after the destruction of their rebuilt temple and the complete overthrow of their country by Titus of Rome. After A.D. 70 they would have no political existence and no temple worship or sacrifices. They would in fact be scattered around the world. But as a people, though in diaspora, they would also maintain a chastened discipline of sorts, eschewing the idolatry that had earlier corrupted them repeatedly.

But the "long time" of the prophecy powerfully implies an end to it as well:

5   **Afterward shall the children of Israel return, and seek the LORD their God, and David their king; and shall fear the LORD and his goodness in the latter days.**

If, in 3:1-5, we see the short-term events of captivity and return, then we also see the long-term prophecy of the diaspora, an even longer captivity, and the reestablishment of Israel, and the subsequent coming of the Messiah-King (for the second time). Hosea would have more easily envisioned the short-term events, but there is a mood in these verses suggesting that he was aware there was more to God's plans than just the next three or four generations.

While this prophecy is focused on the national identity and worship of the Jewish people, the principles inculcated here in Hosea are not without application to Christians. The parallel to the relationship of God's people (or any of her individual persons) to God, is obvious. God's acceptance of the repentant is immediate in Christ; however, to the newly-saved or to the backslidden-penitent, the fullest fellowship with God in which the power and intimate knowledge of him is experienced awaits the establishment of a daily and disciplined walk of fellowship with him.

Chapter 4

The opening chapters of Hosea's prophecy have given his readers an overview of Israel's national unfaithfulness and the big picture of how God will deal with them over both the immediate future and also the upcoming epoch of their dispersion in the world. In chapter 4, Hosea delivers God's specific complaints that eventuated in this national judgment.

Essentially, the theme of the upcoming writing will be that God's people cannot love him in general without obeying him in the specific. Hosea mostly discontinues the metaphor of adultery for the next chapter or so and speaks of specific sins of the people that typify their wayward living and their spiritual deadness.

1 **Hear the word of the LORD, ye children of Israel: for the LORD hath a controversy with the inhabitants of the land, because there is no truth, nor mercy, nor knowledge of God in the land.**

It is often noted that the language of this verse beginning chapter 4 is legal: God brings charges against Israel. "Israel" should be understood here as specifically the northern kingdom. She is charged with lacking three things.

The first is truth *(emet)*. A society can hardly function without its members possessing and exhibiting significant honesty. Where the expectation of one's keeping his word is a toss-up, the paperless contracts of daily living are wrapped in a dark cloud of suspicion, and long-term promises are abandoned because of distrust.

The second charge is that Israel lacks "mercy" (KJV), which is better translated as "love." Love for parents. Love for family. Love of spouse. Love for neighbors. Love of the needy. Love of anyone and everyone other than oneself.

The third charge is "no knowledge of God." It may be easily argued that the previous charges extend from the third. This knowledge *(da'at)* is certainly head-knowledge, but is also heart-knowledge, of the kind that fools hate (Proverbs 1:29), and personal knowledge, so well expressed by Paul in Philippians 3:10: "That I may know him, and the power of his resurrection, and the fellowship of his sufferings, being made conformable unto his death." The Israelites lacked knowledge of the words of the written revelation and also the personal acquaintance of and fellowship with the living God who had inspired that revelation. The law, writings, Psalms and now the prophets provided much of God's revelation they should "know," and showed them how to do so, but they had not committed themselves to living by his word and coming to know him.

2 **By swearing, and lying, and killing, and stealing, and committing adultery, they break out, and blood toucheth blood.**

The lack of truth, love and knowledge was accompanied by, and produced, dishonesty, murder, theft, and rampant adultery. And violence came on in an unbroken stream (**blood toucheth blood**).

This is a horrifying catalog of societal decay. Israel had abandoned God. What once was a nation with a spiritual life was now a people with a mockery of spirituality, directed at non-existent deities.

Modern readers are unwise to fail to apply the image to themselves. The farther from God we live, the more loveless society will be. Interpersonal discord, injustice, crime and violence breed where people acknowledge no absolute values coming from an Almighty God.

3 **Therefore shall the land mourn, and every one that dwelleth therein shall languish, with the beasts of the field, and with the fowls of heaven; yea, the fishes of the sea also shall be taken away.**

Hosea may not have understood his prophecy as referring to some major ecological disaster, certainly not as we think of oil spills and strip mining. But clearly his thought was that God was going to use nature to judge sin.

Human degradation affects people, their country, their economic and political systems, their technology, and ultimately their environment. Certainly man can contribute to his own judgment. But Hosea's words ultimately predicted a divinely orchestrated event.

4   Yet let no man strive, nor reprove another: for thy people are as they that strive with the priest.

The Hebrew of the latter part of this verse is difficult, even confusing. It can be rendered literally, but it doesn't seem to mean anything. The two halves of the verse don't appear to relate. The second phrase, if taken as a conclusion drawn from the first, is a non-sequitur.

The solution may well be that the latter half contains an idiom the meaning of which didn't survive Hosea's era. The first part of the verse seems clear: 'Don't get into arguments with each other over who is to blame.' The second part is: *w ǝamm ǝka kimribe,* which literally is "for your people like those who struggle with the priest." The word for **strive** in the latter part is the same root as in the first part. Most translations dodge the problem and render the phrase literally, letting the reader interpret it as he may.

However, some modern versions infer that the phrase means something more obvious than what its words woodenly say. Thus the ESV says, "for with you is my contention, O priest." And the CSB says, "for my case is against you priests." Thus the GNT's rendering of the entire verse is, "Let no one accuse the people or reprimand *them*—my complaint is against you *priests*" (emphases ours).

What we call "the ministry" today was the priestly class back then, and there were many more of them than career ministers today. The tribe of Levi was variously 1/12 of the population. Not all of them performed the holiest of tasks in the temple. There were many duties, including that of judges, spread throughout the groups of priests. But all of them were leaders in the "spiritual" life of the country. Hosea didn't shy away from indicting "the ministry" for corruption. With plenty of leaders in religion but virtually none in true godliness, was it any wonder the people sank to the bottom of the spiritual and moral barrel?

**5 Therefore shalt thou fall in the day, and the prophet also shall fall
with thee in the night, and I will destroy thy mother.**

"Fall" is *wɔkasal*, "stumble," which includes the implicit idea of
falling as a result. The picture is of people and priests stumbling and
falling in moral and spiritual darkness together, until by God's express
engineering of their national future their "mother"—Israel the nation,
originally intended to be the wife of the divine suitor—is destroyed.

It should be noted that not only the priests as a class but the bulk
of the—self-appointed—prophets are accused and shall be punished.
The writings of the major and minor prophets are evidence of a small
handful of legitimate, God-called men who functioned as his true
prophets in both the southern and northern kingdoms. But there were
many others who thought themselves to be prophets, who proclaimed
messages contrary to those of the divinely called prophets, especially at
the point of holiness to the Lord, strict obedience to the scriptures, and
the foretelling of what God was going to do. Many of them apparently
pooh poohed the idea that God was going to let Israel fall to foreign
powers and go into captivity. And their moral teaching was obviously
not founded on the word of God so-far revealed.

The northern kingdom did not perish for disobeying words of
warning from their "spiritual leaders;" they were brought to an end for
actually following these spiritual role models, who themselves had
plunged into perversion and error. They were like those of whom Jesus
said, "They be blind leaders of the blind. And if the blind lead the blind,
both shall fall into the ditch" (Matthew 15:14).

Having thus narrowed his focus to the priests, under the impress of
the Spirit Hosea gives a more detailed indictment:

**6 My people are destroyed for lack of knowledge: because thou hast
rejected knowledge, I will also reject thee, that thou shalt be no**

priest to me: seeing thou hast forgotten the law of thy God, I will also forget thy children.

The knowledge the people lack is the same "knowledge" *(da'at)* as in v1: they have not been taught the word of God by the priests, and they have not been led to have a spiritual and personal knowledge of the Lord. But the reason is not negligence; the priests themselves have "rejected" knowledge, an intentional act of refusing to believe the word of God as written, to accept its truths and requirements.

Because the priests had abandoned what written word of God they had as the authority for their "ministry," God was going to reject them. They had "forgotten" the law—an act of deliberately displacing it as the authority for their lives and their service, and thus the NIV's, "ignored the law." Accordingly, God would deliberately "forget" about them.

By way of application to the present, this is a picture of the willing ignorance of everyone who hears the truth of God proclaimed and chooses to set it aside and consider anything, everything else in the quest for comfortable or entertaining "truth." But it is especially a portrait of those who have trained for ministry in the word of God and the gospel but who have bought into lies and distortions that have rendered their teachings a useless approximation of spirituality, leading no one to God, but instead leading everyone farther and farther away from the source of salvation and life.

7   **As they were increased, so they sinned against me: therefore will I change their glory into shame.**

As noted previously, "the ministry" class in Israel was defined by the tribe of Levi, and within them the sons of Aaron, so the "increase" was not principally due to population growth—of which there could be expected to be some, of course. Rather, this was an increase in the popularity of the message of "the ministry" in the nation. Baal worship was immensely popular. Idol temple prostitution was popular. The partying atmosphere of the culture was popular. Men already part of the priestly class began leaving the unpopular ministry of teaching a restrictive religion and took up proclaiming the new ideas of syncretistic worship, Baal worship, and lifestyles of "liberated morality" that went along with the culture's discovery of the entertaining world outside Judaism.

But their celebration of perversion and immorality would not last. It would turn to shame and they would not be able to escape the truth that they had bought into lies and promulgated evil.

8   **They eat up the sin of my people, and they set their heart on their iniquity.**

A good translation of "they eat up" (*yokelu*) would be, "They dine on." The popular priest group made a good living promoting things people wanted to hear and wanted to do. Because it worked for them, they doubled down in the espousal of their perverted message. They were careful not to inject any rebuke into their message and leadership. They underwrote the wicked behavior of the populace. After all, it put food on their table.

9   **And there shall be, like people, like priest: and I will punish them for their ways, and reward them their doings.**

Most earlier Bible translations render the first few words of this verse literally, leaving the possibility of two interpretations. One is that the words "like people, like priest" are equivalent to the ageless expression meaning that the second item is similar to the first for *causative* reasons. In other words, because the people are a certain way, the priests are as well. This is a legitimate translation because of the logic of the previous verse. The priests contrived a message of immorality and perversion because that's what the populace wanted to hear. Thus, the priests followed the people before they ostensibly led them. They found a crowd going somewhere and got out in front of it.

The other possible interpretation is that the words are not a common expression at all but a direct statement that the people of Israel as well as their priests—who have just been excoriated—will all be punished alike. This is the sense Holman sees in the verse: "The same judgment will happen to both people and priests." Similarly, the GNT has, "You will suffer the same punishment as the people!"

The second interpretation seems almost too obvious. One can hardly imagine a judgment that would spare one group or the other, intermingled throughout the country. We think the first interpretation is more likely. Those who lead, like those who follow, will suffer the same judgment.

A contemporary application is obvious. The preponderance of evidence about this somewhat difficult text seems to show it to be a scathing indictment of priest and prophet, and less so of the laity they lead. A New Testament caveat would be: "Not many of you should become teachers, my fellow believers, because you know that we who teach will be judged more strictly" (James 3:1).

Several particulars of the indictment are:

(1) The offending preachers are headed for a fall;
(2) One of their chief sins is the failure to know God and to teach the people to know God;
(3) For love of money and by the ease of bilking the gullible out of it, disreputable religious figures have come up with endless schemes to sell a counterfeit of the true word of God.

Hosea would have taken aim at the preacher/prophets who prostitute the ministry for the seductive rewards of notoriety or prosperity. For they hawk a shell of the word of God while milking their hearers for money, refitting their theology to justify it.

10 For they shall eat, and not have enough: they shall commit whoredom, and shall not increase: because they have left off to

take heed to the LORD.

The punishment fits the crime. They dined off the sins of the people, so when God punishes them they will not be able to get enough to eat. They have promoted and become addicted to random, casual, sexual profligacy, so when God punishes them they will see their descendants dry up. It will all be because they have abandoned God.

11 Whoredom and wine and new wine take away the heart.

This proverb, surely meant as a sentence of its own, as the KJV has it, stands in the middle of the prophet's indictment. In addition to the specific, spiritual accusation of leaving God, this "moral of the story" is a lesson even people of little spiritual commitment should be able to agree with, if only from statistical observations.

Hosea had passed along the warning of God in 3:1 that one of the nation's crippling sins was excessive use of intoxicants—"flagons of wine." A flagon was and still is a *large* vessel. Here in 4:11 he generalizes about drinking, and sex—of the non-marital kind. A person who pursues sex as entertainment and alcohol as if it were water will create problems for himself that will often ruin him. A society that does the same destroys the national conscience—"**the heart.**" The love of intoxicating pleasures, whether chemical or sensual, subverts wisdom, clouds reason, and deadens the human soul to the pleadings of the Spirit of God.

A textual issue is interesting in this verse, which itemizes "wine and new wine." The first root word is *ayin,* the familiar word for all products of the grape. The second root word is *tirosh,* which refers to the grape itself or to the boiled-down product, absent most of its water. The process created a paste called must. Normally people diluted it with many parts water for consumption. But people intent on using wine for its inebriating properties would drink it strong.

Perhaps because this was their understanding of the sense of the verse, the translators of the Septuagint used the Greek word μεθυσμα *(methusma)* to render the Hebrew *tirosh. Methusma* specifically means intoxication. Parsing the ancient words for wine and trying to determine whether the specific juice of the grape being spoken of was alcoholic or not is useful study, but there is no debate of what Hosea meant in this context. He meant using alcoholic beverages for their alcoholic properties.

12 My people ask counsel at their stocks, and their staff declareth unto them...

"Stocks" renders a Hebrew word meaning wooden idols. The "staff" was also wooden—worship of Baal and other gods often involved staffs used in divination. Aiming at effecting the poetic content, GNT says, "They ask for revelations from a piece of wood! A stick tells them what they want to know!" The mockery is self-evident.

...for the spirit of whoredoms hath caused them to err, and they have gone a whoring from under their God.

It is not merely prostitution but instead the **spirit** *(ruah)* of prostitution that leads them off into such deep error. This is the same word for "spirit" that is used of the Lord God. We would not be mistaken in assuming that what inspired Israel in this period of intense wickedness was a spiritual entity—probably one of several—that specialized in stirring up sexual deviance and intense desire for fornication. The people had given themselves over to its control.

13 They sacrifice upon the tops of the mountains, and burn incense upon the hills, under oaks and poplars and elms, because the shadow thereof is good...

The "tops of the mountains" were the notorious "high places" established under Jeroboam and successive northern kings, where during periods of quasi-revival under good kings legitimate worship to Yahweh might be offered. Most of the time they were places for pagan worship, which, again, mingled itself with the worship of the Lord all over the northern kingdom. But mountaintops themselves were often rocky. Slightly down the slope a grove of trees made things comfortable. Idol worshipers were interested in pleasure, after all.

Some commentators think the shade was for darkness, to hide shameful acts. This doesn't appear founded on anything in the immediate context or the book as a whole, which forthrightly describes the sins of Israel as open and shameless.

...therefore your daughters shall commit whoredom, and your spouses shall commit adultery.

Both unmarried and the married women engaged in illicit sex in these settings of idol worship, and indeed elsewhere. The term "spouses" is the word for "brides." If a man did decide to marry, there was great likelihood in Israel that his bride would not be sexually pure, and even if she were, there was a good chance she would not be faithful to him.

This indictment of Israelite women for adultery and prostitution did not at all ignore or excuse the men, since obviously both were involved in temple sex and illicit sexual unions everywhere. The symbolism of Hosea's adulterous wife explains some of his concentration on the women of the country and the country itself as the Lord's chosen.

The future scribes and Pharisees would bring to Jesus a woman—just the woman—caught in adultery, as if the man involved were somehow innocent. To make certain that his readers understood that the men of Israel were equally culpable, Hosea delivers this equally weighty warning:

14 **I will not punish your daughters when they commit whoredom, nor your spouses when they commit adultery: for themselves are separated with whores, and they sacrifice with harlots...**

Here again is a little textual confusion. God has already repeatedly announced his judgment on harlotry and adultery. Now, can he actually be saying he won't punish women for these sins?

In an attempt to imply what is not explicitly said in the verse, the CEV has, "But I won't punish them. You men are to blame." The NLT is even more intent on showing how Hosea was evening the balances: "But why should I punish them for their prostitution and adultery? For your men are doing the same thing."

None of the major translations goes so far as to insert modifiers in the verse to suggest that "I will not punish" means anything other than exactly that. But standing where it does in a context of roundly condemning prostitution and adultery, the *force* of the statement is that while God's judgment is going to befall the entire country, men and women included, he is *not* going to *single out* women for punishment, because the men are just as guilty.

Fundamentally, this is a rejection of the double standard of sexual morals. If it's wrong for women, it's wrong for men. Where Israel had gotten in the habit of stoning adulteresses but failing to pursue their consorts, Hosea is saying that to God, both are equally disgraceful. And so the law had made clear long before.

One could even argue cogently that (1) men are to be the leaders of their families and thus of the culture, and (2) it takes both men and women to commit adultery and prostitution, so therefore (3) the punishment of God will befall the men. The women will suffer with them, though not without their own guilt.

...therefore the people that doth not understand shall fall.

The CSB is poignant: "People without discernment are doomed."

In brief summary, the sinful culture of Israel, the northern kingdom, was typified by three things:

(1) Prostitution. The sale of sex was institutionalized, and laws against it were ignored if not forgotten, in the "progressive"

society of Israel.

(2) Alcohol. The use of alcohol (they didn't know what it was, just that it had the desired effect) was prevalent and excessive.

(3) Idolatry. They were caught up in religious practices that were, if they had thought about it, silly; but they didn't think about it.

Added to his condemnation of these specific nationwide sins, God speaks through Hosea to another glaring fault:

15 Though thou, Israel, play the harlot, yet let not Judah offend; and come not ye unto Gilgal, neither go ye up to Bethaven, nor swear, The LORD liveth.

Hosea was concerned—because God was—that Israel's corruption would be rather naturally exported to Judah, for the most obvious reasons. For this reason he gave an explicit warning against Judah's following in Israel's footsteps.

He warned southern kingdom Jews not to go to Gilgal or Bethaven. Both had, in the early history of the conquest and just afterward, been places of blessed encounter with the true God.

Gilgal was where Joshua had the uncircumcised men who had come across the Jordan circumcised and where they all celebrated the Passover before continuing into the region and beginning the conquest of Canaan. But it had come to be a place of idolatry, roundly condemned by Amos (4:4).

Bethel was holy from the time of the patriarchs. There Jacob encountered the Angel of the Lord in his vision of the ladder to heaven, and in ecstasy he named it Beth-El, the house of God. Later he returned to it and encountered God again, renaming the place El Beth-El, the God of the House of God. But Bethel, too, was seized as a place for golden calf worship by Jeroboam, and it was renamed Beth-aven—House of Idols or House of Vanity. Judah was warned not to "go up" to Bethaven, situated on a hill—a "high place."

God further warns Judah—Hosea's writing would circulate to the south—that:

16 Israel slideth back as a backsliding heifer: now the LORD will feed them as a lamb in a large place.

17 Ephraim is joined to idols: let him alone.

Most translators render "backsliding" as "stubborn," which is correct in the modern language, and descriptive to both the ancient and modern mind, to anyone who has herded unruly cattle. Using the same word, Zechariah 7:11 speaks of turning "a stubborn shoulder;" Deuteronomy 21:20 pairs "stubborn and rebellious;" and so, other texts. The KJV translation acquired the sense of falling back from devotion and obedience, and that much was true of Israel, but the core idea of this adjective was their stubbornness in being led in the right way, or being led *back* to that way.

Verse 17 seems a bit confusing in the AV. Almost all other versions see it as a virtual question, as in the NIV's, "How then can the LORD pasture them like lambs in a meadow?" In other words, the sinful state of the nation is such that God cannot simply move on, treating Israel with tenderness and mercy while ignoring her sins. He cannot *lead* her because she will not be led. He cannot *pasture* her because she is a stubborn animal that will not be directed.

18 Their drink is sour: they have committed whoredom continually: her rulers with shame do love, Give ye.

The entire verse is problematic in the original. Holman's translation is especially good, and probably as accurate as it can be: "When their drinking is over, they turn to promiscuity. Israel's leaders fervently love disgrace." The root word for the KJV's **sour is** *sar,* is found elsewhere in the OT as "turned aside," "departed," or "past." The verb somewhat personifies the wine. It has left the cup.

But Israel, like a carousing person, gets up from its empty cup only to go find some sexual encounter to fulfill his thirst for pleasure.

The last phrase is another with textual questions. The Hebrew, translated literally, is simply, "Her rulers dearly love the dishonorable." Whatever the exact idioms or allusions, the sense is that Israel loved its dishonorable behavior over honorable living. The NASB has, "Their rulers dearly love shame."

They loved shame, of course, because they redefined shame as pride. Rejecting the moral code that placed shame on promiscuity, they now saw their behavior as liberating and unconfined. They had redefined terms and concepts so that what had been subject to stigma was now paraded as not only acceptable but also laudable conduct. Thus they were proud of themselves, and they loved what Hosea called shame because their liberated code of conduct gave them license to commit the sins they craved. They did not commit adultery or prostitution or idol sacrifice in a corner or closet, which would imply they accepted the morality of their historical faith. Instead, they reinvented their religion, enabling them to live as they pleased without reproof.

It's vital, of course, to understand the cultural and spiritual dynamics of ancient Israel. Lessons from their particular set of sins, however, beg to be applied to the modern world.

People in the western world and particularly in the United States took with a grain of salt the atheistic preachments of eastern communist countries as they warned their people about the corruption of the west. Russia's and China's political systems were, and are, rife with corruption, in our view. And their official religion, though they deny having any, is the worship of man himself. Ironically, however, they were right about the corruption of the west, at least in moral terms. The United States and Great Britain exported the drug culture through rock music, spread sexual corruption through television and cinema, and disseminated materialism through almost everything else.

This was the concern of Hosea for Judah: don't catch the virus of your sister country's sins. Don't follow their example. Follow the Lord.

19 The wind hath bound her up in her wings, and they shall be ashamed because of their sacrifices.

The irony of this verse is found in its allusion to the description of Israel's beginnings: "I carried you on eagles' wings and brought you to myself" (Exodus 19:4). Now Israel will be cut loose from its moorings in the security of God and will be swept up in the wind of judgment, taken away to a foreign land, dispersed into near nihility like so much scattered chaff.

It would take such drastic judgment, but when it happened, it would dawn on those with any shred of spiritual awareness left in them that their idolatry was to blame, and they would be dearly and deeply **ashamed** by their having made **sacrifices** to Baals. It would be too late for them to reverse the course of their own future and that of the children who were with them in captivity. But perhaps three generations down the road, if they learned the hardest of lessons, they might be able to pass down the fundamental wisdom of following the word of God and worshiping the Lord alone.

Chapter 5

It is almost tiring—if we may say so respectfully—to read the repeated warnings in chapters 1-4. But the prophet probably had the same understanding of the necessity of repetition as the Apostle Paul, who wrote to the Philippian church, "I don't mind repeating what I have written before, and you will be safer if I do so" (Philippians 3:1 GNT). Hosea chapter 5 begins with similar examples of the sins infesting Israel and the judgments that are coming because of them. If the coffin needed more nails, Hosea's prophetic burden, urgent for expression, provided them.

1 **Hear ye this, O priests; and hearken, ye house of Israel; and give ye ear, O house of the king; for judgment is toward you, because ye have been a snare on Mizpah, and a net spread upon Tabor.**

Because of their sins, beginning with priests and extending to every last one who had participated in idolatry, **judgment is toward you,** which is better, "is against you," or even, "is coming for you." The Hebrew has simply, "is yours." And why? It is because places such as **Mizpah** and **Tabor** have displayed the rank idolatry and perversion of the country.

Mizpah was where long ago Jacob and Laban made a covenant of mutual respect and watchful warning, setting up a pile of stones and calling it Mizpah—"watchtower."

Mizpah was where Samuel had headquartered his prophetic judgment over Israel, where after a defeat of the Philistines by God's power Samuel set up stones and called the place Ebenezer —"Hitherto has the Lord helped us."

Now **Mizpah,** a historic reminder of the journey of the patriarch and the providential victory of God, had become an infamous place of idol worship.

Tabor is a mountain in Israel where Barak, under the inspired judge Deborah, battled Canaanite kings and subdued them. It was where Gideon executed the Midianite kings who had killed his brothers. It was a place of victory recalling God's presence and power with Israel.

Now, **Tabor** had become a high place of the grossest idol worship and prostitution.

What made this corruption worse was that the leaders, the **priests** and the **house of the king**, had **snared** the people into it by leading the way.

2   **And the revolters are profound to make slaughter, though I have been a rebuker of them all.**

Some of the versions have "depravity" for "slaughter" *(wəsahatah)*, but the prevailing meaning throughout the OT is "slaughter," and so KJV, NIV, ESV, CSV and others. The word is evocative of the slaughter of sacrifice to Baals. However, it is not merely the slaughter of animals that is condemned—God's own worship involved frequent animal sacrifice at the temple. Rather, here the context includes the uselessness of the loss of life because of the falseness of the gods. And it should be noted that Baal worship sometimes involved the sacrifice of children.

The KJV's **revolters** is more familiar to the modern ear as "rebels," and refers to the nature of idolatry for the Israelite: it was at heart rebellion against all that God had ever commanded.

3   **I know Ephraim, and Israel is not hid from me: for now, O Ephraim, thou committest whoredom, and Israel is defiled.**

Ephraim was sometimes used as a representative name for Israel, having been the name of the second son of Joseph, but the one blessed with priority by Jacob (Genesis 48:14). Ephraim's was the tribe of Joshua, who led the whole of Israel to victory in conquering Canaan. Ephraim had a storied past and a great heritage. For Ephraim to lead the way in idolatry and prostitution was the height of disgrace.

4   **They will not frame their doings to turn unto their God: for the**

spirit of whoredoms is in the midst of them, and they have not known the LORD.

Literally translated, the LXX has, ουκ εδωκαν τα διαβουλια— "They did not give their counsel" to return to God. Most versions have "permit" or "allow" for "give counsel." The sense seems to be that if they heard Hosea and other genuine prophets, they simply ignored the word of God in those prophets' preaching because they were too wrapped up in their pleasure. They didn't even make any attempt to course-correct. There was no conscience left in them. Their spirits were not the least touched by the message of rebuke and warning. As Ecclesiastes 8:11 says, "the heart of the sons of men is fully set in them to do evil."

The description of the **spirit of whoredoms** being **in the midst of them** is not merely idiomatic. What possessed the country and all those in it who were swept along in the tide of idol worship was an actual spiritual being, an evil spirit who inspired worship of a false god and who stirred up perverse longings in them, to be fulfilled in rampant immorality. These spirits were abroad in the nations surrounding Israel, and would be dealt with eventually by the One who came to defeat the principalities and powers (Colossians 2:15). They were the spiritual powers that rebelled shortly after the foundation of the world, infesting the earth before the flood and again after it, turning the hearts of men toward the worship of self and sensuality, centered in a "god" who epitomized these things.

5   **And the pride of Israel doth testify to his face: therefore shall Israel and Ephraim fall in their iniquity; Judah also shall fall with them.**

Their **pride**—arrogance—is self evident and condemns them. Their sins did not need to be uncovered; nothing needed finding out. They wore their indecent, obscene and unholy lives like banners. When their end came, there would be no excuse. And Judah would be not far behind.

6   **They shall go with their flocks and with their herds to seek the
    LORD; but they shall not find him; he hath withdrawn himself
    from them.**

Hosea looked out into the near future and predicted that when the
waves of God's punishment began to be felt, there might be a
movement by some to appease the Lord. Perhaps a few people in Israel
who had tried to maintain some kind of faithfulness to the ancient
traditions would invoke this response. But even with a flood of
sacrifices to the Lord, unaccompanied by genuine repentance and
offered too late, they would not find him at the place of atonement.

7   **They have dealt treacherously against the LORD: for they have
    begotten strange children: now shall a month devour them with
    their portions.**

Strange children is literally "illegitimate," and we should first
consider this as one of their social problems. A land littered with
prostitutes and their clients and having little to no birth control methods
would be populated with illegitimate children.

Life in contemporary cultures offers a parallel in the widespread
disregard of the moral implications of rampant illegitimacy. It should go
without saying that no blame should rest on children born to anyone
other than married parents. But western societies are approaching a
point at which bearing children only within marriage is no longer the
accepted, desired norm. People who shed their parents' morality to live
in sexual "freedom" do not often pass along holy sexual morals to their
children. Those children in turn have no fixed values to teach to their
own children, a greater number of whom are raised by choice in single-
parent homes.

The literal problem of illegitimacy in Ephraim was made worse by
what was signified by it: they were pagan (NKJV and Amplified). In the

plan of God, families rear children "in the nurture and admonition of the Lord" (Ephesians 6:4) and those children, brought into a genuine relationship with God as they grow up, repeat the pattern with their own families, and so on. But when a generation generally, as a whole, fails to rear its children to worship the Lord God, the God of the Bible, leaving those children to the tender mercies of a pagan society (in the ancient day) or a godless society (in our own day), there remains little hope for the future of that people.

Month is literally "new moon." Many modern translators think this was a specific prophecy of something befalling Israel during a (particular?) New Moon festival. If the Israelites, or at least some of them, were going through the motions of New Moon festivals in the first place, it was evidently along with Baal worship. If no festival is meant, the term suggests a short period of time, though not necessarily literally a month.

The encapsulated message of God through Hosea said that eventually God wanted to restore Israel, to reclaim her. But first, judgment must come.

As part of their judgment, Israel was to fall prey to land-grabbers among the princes of Judah, whom God encouraged to indulge themselves.

8   **Blow ye the cornet in Gibeah, and the trumpet in Ramah: cry aloud at Bethaven, after thee, O Benjamin.**

The **cornet** and **trumpet,** then as today, are similar instruments, the cornet a bit smaller. Both were used to call alarms and alert people to defense. The mention of **Benjamin** shows that Judah was ultimately also in the cross hairs of external enemies.

Later, Assyria would finish off both of them, though the northern kingdom, Israel, would never again arise. Judah would reappear after captivity, and her Davidic kingly line would be fulfilled in Jesus Christ.

9   Ephraim shall be desolate in the day of rebuke…

The northern kingdom would suffer the kind of invasion and attack that would be indefensible when it came.

…among the tribes of Israel have I made known that which shall surely be.

'Don't say later that I did not warn you.' **Surely be** is a guarantee. These are no empty warnings, no mere likelihoods. These are not predictions, but statements of fact, envisioning what God already sees because he is timeless, is in all times, and sees all times, all the time.

10   The princes of Judah were like them that remove the bound: therefore I will pour out my wrath upon them like water.

Deuteronomy 19:14 had long ago prohibited the occasional thievery of land by moving boundary stones (not altogether removing them). Deuteronomy 27:17 pronounced a curse on anyone who did it.

The religious equivalent was what Hosea sought to symbolize. Israel's leaders—the **priests** and **house of the king** as earlier mentioned—had led the way in redefining the moral laws. Common thieves steal surreptitiously. The **princes** who pervert the laws of God do so out in the open, shamelessly, as if they had the authority to define right and wrong. The charge is not paired with specific incidents. Where such things develop in formerly strongly religious societies, the redefinition involves distancing themselves from the requirements of laws because of the "antiquity" of those laws. They were old fashioned and therefore discarded.

11   Ephraim is oppressed and broken in judgment, because he willingly walked after the commandment.

Commandment is "precept" in the Hebrew, but overwhelmingly the versions take it to refer to human standards of right and wrong, not God's. The LXX has "vain things." Thus the NASB, "man's command;" CSB, "what is worthless;" and Amplified, "man's command (vanities, filth, secular precepts)." The significant thing about this charge is that the northern Israelites were not merely rebelling against God's law, but redefining it (as in v10).

12 Therefore will I be unto Ephraim as a moth, and to the house of Judah as rottenness.

Like a **moth** eats away in the darkness and decay (**rottenness**) breaks down flesh and other formerly living things, so God's judgment will be—and already was—seen in the unstoppable deterioration of Israel's moral fiber. It would not be able to sustain its cultural life or its political existence under the divinely ordained onslaught of this decay.

13 When Ephraim saw his sickness, and Judah saw his wound, then went Ephraim to the Assyrian, and sent to king Jareb: yet could he not heal you, nor cure you of your wound.

Sickness and **wound** are metaphors for Israel's worsening political situation, a weakened government threatened by her eastern neighbors.

Jareb is of uncertain meaning. It appears again in 10:6. The lemma means "let him contend," suggesting "King Contention." One of today's fictional heros might well have been used in this way if Hosea's message were contemporary; Jareb was apparently any "Superman" Ephraim might have begged to come help him.

Mixing metaphors, Hosea said a king of combat couldn't heal Israel of its wound. As in other prophetic writings, God warned Judah and Israel not to turn to any surrounding nation to solve its problems, but instead to turn to and trust him. When they didn't, they eventually regretted their alliances and were reprimanded for them.

14 For I will be unto Ephraim as a lion, and as a young lion to the house of Judah: I, even I, will tear and go away; I will take away, and none shall rescue him.

The KJV has **young lion** as do many other versions, though the NIV has "great lion." The point it that it was a strong, young lion rather than an old one. The young lion is eager to prove his hunting ability and is brash and strong. The image is of a capable enemy totally overwhelming Israel, to her complete demise. And like a lion or other predatory cat often makes a kill and carries away the prey with its jaws around the dying animal's neck, so Israel and Judah in turn would be carried away for the enemy to devour.

15 **I will go and return to my place, till they acknowledge their offence, and seek my face: in their affliction they will seek me early.**

Now, God himself is the lion, returning to his **place,** which mixes in the imagery with a lion's lair. If we should assign a specific meaning to this **place** it would simply be his continual abode. He reaches out with his disciplining hand—or "paw," if we retain the image—and when he has done to Israel what he promised, he withdraws and waits for them to be brought to their senses and repent.

Seek me early is a bit misleading if taken literally in the English. In today's parlance, it would be "earnestly." So NIV, ESV and others. CSB has "in their distress," which is reasonable. The Hebrew *yəsaharunni* means "they will earnestly seek me," as in Proverbs 1:28, where it is similarly translated "diligently." It will be to no avail.

Israel's political solutions would not solve its spiritual problems, nor those of any nation since, no matter how great its heritage of faith in God.

Many commentators think, as we do, that the first three verses of chapter 6 belong with chapter 5. They nicely round out the thoughts of the chapter and show what Hosea projected as the appropriate response of Ephraim to what was happening and what was going to eventuate in the nation. However, the dual nature of many prophecies' fulfillment was nowhere more needed than here, for the short term salvation of the nation was not to be. In the long term, however, a salvation was coming that would fulfill the national hope. Meanwhile, the prophet looked at the sad situation before him.

Chapter 6

Chapters 6-7 mark a turning point in the book of Hosea, both in the "tone of God's voice," and in the metaphors Hosea uses for Israel. Prior to this point, Israel has been the wife of the LORD, who has been unfaithful to him. Now Hosea begins regularly to call Israel "Ephraim," and refers to him as the child of God, a son to him.

Chapter 6 begins with Ephraim speaking, or Israelites talking to other Israelites, responding to the prophecies of Hosea and others calling them to repent. The first three verses are a wonderful expression of the intent to repent, and the faith that the LORD will receive, forgive and heal them.

1 **Come, and let us return unto the LORD: for he hath torn, and he will heal us; he hath smitten, and he will bind us up.**

If Israel looked back in her united national memory she (or "he," to be consistent with Jacob/Israel here) would recall many events of divine discipline and restoration. There were periods of sin and repentance in the wilderness before they even entered the Promised Land. They had a history of God's redemptive activity being needed and received. Their hope now, in this national crisis, was that there was yet one redemptive episode in God's plan.

2 **After two days will he revive us: in the third day he will raise us up, and we shall live in his sight.**

It is tempting for the Christian to see a prophetic allusion to the resurrection of Christ. In fact some early church commentators held this view. But it has little to recommend it when the language is studied without prejudice. **After two days** was an expression for "tomorrow," and **the third day** was a way of representing a short time, though not necessarily of any exact number of days—or even hours. The GNT, recognizing this, compacts the language: "In two or three days he will revive us..."

The point of the verse is that the Israelites were gearing up to be hopeful that if they just said the right things to God, trying to show some seriousness in returning to worship of him, he would halt all his plans of judgment and feel sorry for them. The evidence that this "repentance" —though pitifully expressed—was too little and too late, is that when they completed their hopeful thoughts, God continued (v4) to lament their hypocrisy and shallowness.

3   **Then shall we know, if we follow on to know the LORD: his going forth is prepared as the morning; and he shall come unto us as the rain, as the latter and former rain unto the earth.**

Again, at first glance, this appears to be a hopeful quotation by Hosea, a note of repentance in the midst of judgment. Taken that way, it would have been a tremendous expression of faith: that salvation will come from the one who has judged, and restoration from the one who had cast away. After all, who but God can save? Once smitten, can any but God eternally heal? Whether or not God will relent in his judgment, however, depends entirely on the sincerity and persistence of repentance, whether—as John the Baptist put it—those who claim to repent also produce fruits worthy of repentance (Luke 3:8).

Israel's "turning" to God would not result in deliverance this time; rather, judgment would befall them without any relenting. Nevertheless, "they" express a genuine prayer of devotion and godly faith —or at least, this was Hosea's version of what should be the earnest plaintiveness of their collective hearts. "Let us acknowledge the Lord" (NIV). The Hebrew has wənedəah, "And let us know." It is a prediction of knowing the Lord *if* they **follow on** or "pursue" the knowledge of him. They are urging themselves to be committed to knowing their true God.

Remember that these are not the words of any representative group of Israel's citizens responding to Hosea's preaching. This is Hosea putting words in their mouths, not in ridicule but by way of envisioning what he wished in his deepest heart were their response.

There is much made of the **latter and former rain** in some Christian theories, some seeing the latter rain as end-time revival in the church, paired with a great influx of "all Israel," meaning those who are sons of Abraham by faith. The expression occurs in Joel 2:23 in much the same context, that of the return of the blessings of weather that restores a land parched with drought. There, more than here, some have seen a future fulfillment in terms of spiritual blessings. Matthew Henry acknowledges the belief but does not give any stress to it himself. Most commentators note the weaknesses of the view.

The question for purposes of our application is whether or not 6:1-3 are Hosea's giving voice to the plea of the very few left in the northern kingdom who joined him in a passionate prayer to God, *or* if these are words Israel *could have* uttered but didn't. If the latter, as we have suggested above, then the application of the expectation of the Lord's coming to them **as the latter and former rain** is to be found in assurances that, by whatever means of deprivation God has judged, he will restore in kind.

Verse 3 contains the standard by which genuine repentance is judged: "If we follow on to know the LORD (KJV)." Like one of the brothers in Jesus' parable (Matthew 21:28-31), so many say, "I will," but don't.

The reader of this passage does well to accompany it with a sigh throughout. God lists more of Israel's sins, but with ineffable sadness.

4 **O Ephraim, what shall I do unto thee? O Judah, what shall I do unto thee? for your goodness is as a morning cloud, and as the early dew it goeth away.**

Regardless of the theoretical prayer of a hypothetical Israelite responding to the warnings of the prophet, the answer of the very real God is denial of the request. If the idea of returning rains is hopeless, then the **goodness** (better, "love" or "loyalty") of Ephraim and Judah, too, is measured by the same idiom: it is like a **cloud** that seems to promise rain, but dissipates in the morning sun, as does the **dew.**

To apply this truth contemporarily on a large scale, consider a godly people in a culture who profess great commitment to the Lord but who compromise with the ungodly all around them. On a smaller scale, think in terms of individuals whose morning prayers, perhaps hastily uttered, are quickly lost in the heat of the day's activities—promises never kept and commitments not honored.

5   **Therefore have I hewed them by the prophets; I have slain them by the words of my mouth: and thy judgments are as the light that goeth forth.**

God speaks to Hosea, brings into the prophet's mind the imagery of the Lord himself as the lumberjack and the prophets as the axes, felling those who rebelliously and resolutely sin. Some versions render **light** *(owr)* as "lightning," which is appropriate, its being the only light that **goeth forth** that we encounter. The KJV has **judgments** as do almost all other versions; however, it is not merely a "guilty" or "not guilty" verdict that constitutes this judgment. It is the laying down of the law, a full explanation of why the people's sins *are* sins, and why they are so indefensible and worthy of condemnation. It is not that God has not previously declared what is just and what is not, but rather that God pairs his punishment with incontrovertible explanations that will leave the guilty with no excuse and no defense.

6   **For I desired mercy, and not sacrifice; and the knowledge of God more than burnt offerings.**

To love God (**mercy**) and to know him, as ideally the Israelite depicted in 6:1-3 would have done, was God's goal for his people. Without these things, the sacrifices they offered were empty symbols unmatched with holy and devoted living. **Mercy** *(hesed)* is often rendered "lovingkindness." It doesn't depend on circumstances in which someone deserves discipline but receives undeserved benevolence.

Rather, this mercy is the daily and continual conduct of love, inspired by the character of God.

7 But they like men have transgressed the covenant: there have they dealt treacherously against me.

Notice the poignant reference that isn't seen in the KJV. **Like men** *(kəadam)* in the King James is, we believe, rendered "like Adam" (ESV, NLT, NASB and others). The story of Adam in Genesis is not just an account of man's fall into sin. It is also the story of God's broken-heartedness about Adam. Time is nothing to God, of course; but here, millennia after Adam, God speaks to and through Hosea, and Adam is on his mind. His heart is still affected by Adam's breaking of the first covenant, his souring of Eden's perfection, his introduction of death into the world. Adam, after his wife but as head of them both, officially started the spiral to destruction. How God's heart has ached since!

8 Gilead is a city of them that work iniquity, and is polluted with blood.

The mention of **Gilead** takes the reader back to the battle of Judge Deborah against Jabin, king of Canaan, whose armies were led by the famed Sisera. As Deborah and Barak mustered an army, Makir the son of Manasseh and the father of Gilead, the man, hunkered down in their own country rather than join Deborah and Barak (himself afraid to take the lead) in the fight. And yet we learn from biblical history that Makir's sons—which would have included Gilead—were "great soldiers" (Joshua 17:1, NIV). Deborah and Barak went to war with what they had. After it was over and Israel had won, Deborah's song pointed out the hesitation—or dare we say cowardice—of Gilead in not coming to the aid of the other tribes.

Later, Gilead was a retreat from impending battle for some of the Hebrews in the time of King Saul (1 Samuel 13:7). God still claimed Gilead as his (Psalm 60:7), representing the eastern tribes, and it tended to receive the general weal or woe of the nation at large.

Most Christians' familiarity with Gilead is from the song based on Jeremiah 8:22 referring to "a balm in Gilead." This phrase, in all probability, comes from the main export of Gilead which was gum of the terebinth used throughout the region to create medicinal salve.

Now this territory of retreat, first of reticence and gradually of benefit to its brother tribes, was a veritable center of sin and a place of fearful bloodshed. All the places in God's holy land that had been known for his blessing or goodness or salvation were now becoming synonymous with the rankest of wickedness, in imitation of the vile nations around them that God had disgorged in order to give them to his people of choice.

9   **And as troops of robbers wait for a man, so the company of priests murder in the way by consent: for they commit lewdness.**

Robbers are expected to be robbers, and there are robbers in every land in every era. However, no one expects, or no one should expect, priests to act like robbers. Yet Hosea says that there were bands of priests murdering in the hilly road to Shechem, probably the road that led to Jerusalem to the south. The KJV takes the noun *sekmah* in its root meaning and renders it **by consent**, but this is surely a reference to Shechem—ironically an official city of refuge. And it was no metaphorical accusation. It was a startling and outrageous reality. Some of those who were called to be priests were quite actually predators. The reader may justly make a contemporary application by expanding the concept of predation.

10   **I have seen an horrible thing in the house of Israel: there is the whoredom of Ephraim, Israel is defiled.**

Nearly all the versions have **horrible,** though the NET Bible has "disgusting." The sense of the utterance is that a word did not exist that sufficiently describe how abominable the state of immorality and lawlessness was in the northern kingdom.

11 Also, O Judah, he hath set an harvest for thee

    A period belongs at the end of this phrase, where the AV has the sentence continue. Almost all translators agree that the next phrase belongs with 7:1. The **harvest** spoken of, then, is a "harvest of punishment" (NLT). The Amplified's bracketed explanation is "[of divine judgment]."

Chapter 7

The poignancy of the situation in the northern kingdom continues as God bemoans the obstinacy and redoubled rebellion of his people against decency, law, love, faith, or any other semblance of godliness:

1   When I would have healed Israel, then the iniquity of Ephraim was discovered, and the wickedness of Samaria: for they commit falsehood; and the thief cometh in, and the troop of robbers spoileth without.

Another good example of anthropomorphic speech is here, as God is planning healing when he "discovers" the sin of Ephraim and Samaria. **Discover** in the text *(wəniglah* - "was uncovered"*)* is the usual word for the quite human experience of coming to know something one didn't know before. God doesn't surprisingly discover anything, of course. The sin uncovered was **falsehood,** which is *saqer*, or fraud, and two kinds of thievery: burglary and robbery. The terms encompass the range of stealing. Theirs was a crime-ridden society.

2   And they consider not in their hearts that I remember all their wickedness: now their own doings have beset them about; they are before my face.

The observation the prophet makes, as the Spirit speaks through him, is that God's people have come to the point in the poverty of their understanding of him that they do not live with any apparent awareness of the omniscience of the Lord. People who neglect God soon believe he is not there to see them. While hiding one's deeds from other people is sometimes easy, it is impossible to hide them from God. And while most people pass their entire lives with thoughts and beliefs that remain completely private, unknown to any other human being, those things, too, are an open book to the Almighty.

Further, God never forgets, not in any sense involving his omniscience. **I remember,** he says through Hosea. While he may intentionally *disregard* the sins he forgives, he does not lose the consciousness of anything he knows, which includes Israel's sins. **Before my face** employs the word *panay,* which means face, sight, countenance, presence—everything the face of a person suggests in the way of the senses and the personality.

3   They make the king glad with their wickedness, and the princes with their lies.

The root word of **glad** is *samǝch,* which in this context suggests the idea of "entertained." The accusation was as much against the king and princes, who enjoyed the goings on in the country, as it was against the doers.

4   They are all adulterers, as an oven heated by the baker, who ceaseth from raising after he hath kneaded the dough, until it be leavened.

Generally recognized as one of the difficult passages of Hosea, Chapter 7:4-9 introduces the illustration of bread and bread making as an image of the developing sinful culture in Israel. In turn, each of the elements of the picture represents Ephraim, or Israel, in some aspect of their sin. Note in these verses that now Ephraim the man-nation, a male, is seen as an adulterer, or a nation of adulterers. This is apparently meant both literally and figuratively.

The symbol is not of sexual lusts only. They were hot tempered as well. This prophecy probably dates to the time right before the accession of Hoshea to the throne (2 Kings 15:30) and the assassination of Pekah. There was a rapid succession of kings, who reigned each for a matter of months on the average. Politics was a game of passions. What men of greed and lust for power wanted, they grabbed for, using whatever means was necessary.

Hosea's message was first that they were aflame from the inside with everything evil and nothing good. First, they are the **oven** itself, which has been stoked and is hot, as Israel's people are overheated with sexual lust and every other kind of passion.

The baker kneading the dough is possibly simply an agent in the story who carries the action along. And yet he is involved in an odd way shortly.

Skipping temporarily to v6:

6   For they have made ready their heart like an oven, whiles they lie in wait: their baker sleepeth all the night; in the morning it burneth as a flaming fire.

7   They are all hot as an oven, and have devoured their judges; all their kings are fallen: there is none among them that calleth unto me.

8   Ephraim, he hath mixed himself among the people; Ephraim is a cake not turned.

The story of the baker skips to verse 6, where the **oven** is again the heart of the sinner. In the same verse, the **baker** leaves the oven overnight and resumes his task in the morning. When he does, he is drawn into the oven (CSB). Some versions, following the LXX, take the Hebrew to mean the baker is consumed by the fire he himself over-stoked. The baker here may represent the **judges** and the **kings** who also **are fallen**—victims of perhaps a hot tempered people.

This leads us to the statement of v7 that **They are all hot as an oven,** which the range of commentators take to be yet another metaphor for the people's burning passion and licentiousness. On the heals of this charge, the prophet says **Ephraim** has **mixed himself among the people.** The CSB says, "has allowed himself to get mixed up with the nations," which clarifies the condemnation. Israel was supposed to be holy *unto the Lord.* It was to be a peculiar people, a people set apart. It was precisely "mixing with the nations" that defined the epitome of wrongdoing for them.

Whether connected to this accusation or not, the short charge (v8) that Ephraim was **a cake unturned** ends the imagery of the baker. The

cake is the flat cake or flatbread typical to the middle east for thousands of years. Its not being turned suggests an interruption of the intended process, and the ruination of the cake, since it would be burned on one side. What this means is of varied opinions, but it communicates what we mean when we say, "half baked." Israel interrupted the process of her development as God's people, by departing from the LORD. She, or he (here, as Ephraim), is therefore unappealing, ruined, fit for the fire, not the palate.

Completing the illustration of the baker and the bread, we must then consider 7:5, which, at least subject-wise, was interjected:

5   **In the day of our king the princes have made him sick with bottles of wine; he stretched out his hand with scorners.**

It is uncertain which **king** is meant, though it may not matter. The **princes** would be the literal princes or the various other persons at the royal court. The image is of their getting the king drunk to the point of being sick. But whether **stretching out his hand with scorners** means toasting each other is uncertain. The entire picture is a bit confusing without the particulars that the contemporary reader would have known, or without better understanding of the figures of speech. Most of the translations render the words as strictly as possible and leave it to the reader to interpret as led.

9   **Strangers have devoured his strength, and he knoweth it not: yea, gray hairs are here and there upon him, yet he knoweth not.**

The next illustration Hosea employs is that of a man who is older than he thinks himself to be, in spite of the number of his years. Men in particular are reluctant to admit the deleterious effects of age on their bodies and occasionally to attempt things they are beyond being able to perform anymore. Here, Ephraim's **strength,** which he thinks is still like he had in his prime, alas, has been **devoured**, or sapped (NIV) by "foreigners" (CSB).

The word for **strangers** is *zarim,* which can be translated "aliens," and means foreign nationals. It would be tempting to read back into the text an understanding of troubles experienced by a modern country from especially the excessive presence of foreign nationals in its economy, but it isn't likely that any economic impact of foreigners is meant here. Certainly the chief thing meant is that foreign nations brought their religions into Israel, confusing new generations of Israelite children, influencing the impressionable, and infecting the culture of the worship of the Lord with all the abominable idol-worship of the rest of the world. It was this confusion and dilution of the worship of the true God that weakened the nation.

Not only has Ephraim's strength been sapped, but he's turning **gray** and tells himself he isn't. Hosea takes a snapshot of a man over the upper edge of his prime, who is unaware that his virility is waning and is insufficient for the task. Israel boasts of its prowess in the world community, unaware that it is about to be taken down not just a peg or two, but the whole distance, by a pagan power.

In the midst of his declining powers, Ephraim redoubles his boast of manhood:

10 And the pride of Israel testifieth to his face: and they do not return to the LORD their God, nor seek him for all this.

The **pride** spoken of is Israel's arrogant belief that nothing was fatally amiss about their country, that they were still well able to perform as a "world" power. The signs of their impotence were in front of their face, but they would not admit their sins and their predicament and seek God for healing and renewal.

11 Ephraim also is like a silly dove without heart: they call to Egypt, they go to Assyria.

A **dove**, often used in scripture as a symbol of innocence or purity, is employed here to suggest someone witless or easily deceived. Perhaps these are in some sense the inverse of the complimentary qualities, which is what deep and continual sinfulness tends to do. **Without heart** *(en leb)* is without good sense. Israel, whose leaders are easily deceived—perhaps because of desperation—turned to more powerful surrounding nations **Egypt** and **Assyria** to help them, the latter of which desired only to engulf and devour them. Perhaps this was an early illustration of the Stockholm Syndrome.

12 **When they shall go, I will spread my net upon them; I will bring them down as the fowls of the heaven; I will chastise them, as their congregation hath heard.**

This verse simply continues the imagery of 7:12. Here, Israel is not merely one dove but a flock, which the birder catches at the opportune moment. God will punish them just as he said he would. What **their congregation hath heard** was the prophecy predicting their downfall—Hosea's prophecy and that of any other genuine prophet who had told them what was going to happen. It was necessary to tell them *now* to remember *later* that they had been warned. For as Hosea spoke and they caught wind of his message, they were inclined to dismiss his warnings. What nation, doubling down on their sinful direction, listens to preachers, who always seem to be condemning something?

13 **Woe unto them! for they have fled from me: destruction unto them! because they have transgressed against me: though I have redeemed them, yet they have spoken lies against me.**

God intends to punish them for straying and rebelling (**fled from me**), and for speaking **lies** about him. These lies were likely statements of beliefs based on their conclusions about God. These lies would have replaced the holy confessions of faith that characterized their faithful forebears. The "problem of evil," for instance, which as a philosophical argument against the existence of God has been around for millennia, may have been answered by them with a flat denial of the existence of Yahweh, or else a denial of his power or providence or goodness.

The lies need not have been official written statements. They may simply have been the prevailing statements of policy by kings and princes, especially those reversing or perverting longstanding statements of God's law. Perhaps the greatest of their lies was found in their insistence that the LORD was not the only god they could or should worship. After all, the Baals and Ashtoreth for the Canaanites, Astarte, Molech, Dagon, Marduk, and others for the Phonecians and residents of Ur, all the Egyptian gods and goddesses—didn't they predate the revelation of Yahweh to Abraham, the Israelites might have said? And aren't they all regional gods? And isn't it wise to pay them all respect? Soon the questions would have become confident assertions of the Israelite society, and therefore lies.

Today's lies of this sort would include: the pernicious falsehood that gender is not a defining part of a person as conceived and born, but rather chosen later; the convenient reversal of scientific fact denying that a person is a human being from the moment of conception; the claim that human sexual expression has no moral tie to the establishment of marriage but is the right of every person dependent only on consent; and the insistence that homosexual behavior is not a sin and that homosexuality is a trait from birth, despite there being no scientific evidence for such a claim. These lies are purveyed in order to justify perversion and violence.

14 And they have not cried unto me with their heart, when they howled upon their beds...

The picture the prophet draws is of the nation's people going to bed with a painful, pervasive sense of the futility of their lives, day after day, spent in the quest for pleasure but ever deepening in emptiness. Some or many of them may have cried themselves to sleep over the repeated wasted-ness of their lives. But this sorrow was not "godly sorrow unto repentance" (2 Corinthians 7:10) but something far short of it. Instead of crying out to the darkness, they should have called out to the light, the Lord God.

…they assemble themselves for corn and wine, and they rebel against me.

The Hebrew is confusing, and possibly some compact allusions are at fault. The NIV has an indication of self-abusive worship: "They slash themselves, appealing to their gods for grain and new wine." Holman and the ESV follow. The problem seems to be the word *yitgowraru,* which the King James's translators rendered "they assemble," but which several later translators took to mean "cut themselves," based on the Septuagint and a few Hebrew manuscripts. In turn, those translations were influenced by ancient scholars who believe a single letter in the Hebrew word had been miscopied—a daleth to a resh. If we are less concerned with the probably insoluble issue of a miscopied letter than we are with the simpler question of what the Israelites **assembled** themselves for, the answer is more certain. Why would they assemble, and before whom, and what would they do? Knowing that they were worshiping Baal, one may assume this was the case in this verse, that they were assembling before a Baal image to entreat the god for a good harvest. Knowing that Baal worshipers frequently cut themselves in worship (e.g. 1 Kings 18:28), we may also assume this was implied in their assembly, to show their sincere desperation. The prophet's point was that they were going to the wrong god.

15 **Though I have bound and strengthened their arms, yet do they imagine mischief against me.**

Nearly all the versions translate the Hebrew word meaning "disciplined" as "trained" instead of the KJV's "**bound**." They were attempting to turn against God all he had done for them. None of this conduct made sense. It defied wisdom.

16 They return, but not to the most High…

The question poses itself, to whom did they return if not to the Most High? The answer lies in taking the Hebrew *yasubu* as "turn" instead of "return." They turned around, looking for someplace else to go, some answer to their predicament, but they didn't go back to God. He was the one to whom they *should* have turned, but they didn't. As the NLT puts it, "They look everywhere except to the Most High."

…they are like a deceitful bow…

Better, "a faulty bow." Whether the bow represents them or one or more of their strategies to regain national prominence and strength is not developed in the image. Archery is a difficult skill to begin with, but even a good archer can't do much with a broken or faulty bow. The image is of an unstrung or too loosely strung bow, useless in battle. The idea is that someone startled and turning to defend himself draws back his bow but due to some defect in it he cannot shoot straight or at all, and is thus overwhelmed by the enemy. Israel didn't have what it took to survive the testing of God.

…their princes shall fall by the sword for the rage of their tongue: this shall be their derision in the land of Egypt.

Hosea cites the **rage** of the princes' tongues—the curses they have uttered *(mizza'am)*—as the specific sin for which they would be punished appropriately by the **derision** of **Egypt**.

Chapter 8

Where chapters 6-7 were written mostly in the sad tone of a God grieving over his wayward child, chapter 8 is full of growing resolve devoid of the constraints of compassion. There is nothing to do but to bring Israel to an end, to overrun her with enemies. They have brought such consequences on themselves.

1 **Set the trumpet to thy mouth. He shall come as an eagle against the house of the LORD, because they have transgressed my covenant, and trespassed against my law.**

The **trumpet** was sounded for battle, and Hosea was instructed to sound it—certainly through the notes of his preaching. **He** is the **LORD** himself, like an eagle swooping down for its prey. It was time for judgment to fall because of the surpassing transgression of the chosen people.

2 **Israel shall cry unto me, My God, we know thee.**

They will say to Hosea and into the air hoping to reach God—but we *know* you! You are our God! But as long as they thought of him as one among many, to be given equal time but not sole worship, he was *not* their God.

What follows is a summary assessment of the reason they are about to be destroyed.

3 **Israel hath cast off the thing that is good: the enemy shall pursue him.**

It is too late. The **good** cast off cannot be recovered. They are left to the enemy.

4 **They have set up kings, but not by me: they have made princes, and I knew it not: of their silver and their gold have they made them idols, that they may be cut off.**

5 **Thy calf, O Samaria, hath cast thee off; mine anger is kindled**

against them: how long will it be ere they attain to innocency?
6   **For from Israel was it also: the workman made it; therefore it is not God: but the calf of Samaria shall be broken in pieces.**

Note how many of these things have their roots in the early days of Israel's existence: they broke the covenant in the wilderness; they built a golden calf as an idol, also in the wilderness; they demanded a king in Canaan, when God didn't wish them to have one. All these early sins of the nation reappear and haunt them.

Two interpretations can be put forth for v5, depending on how the Hebrew *zanah* ("is rejected") is read. The KJV takes its reading from the Masoretic text and translates the verb straight, where **calf** is the subject and **cast off** the verb. The sense would then be that if the **calf** (or calves) they made had been, in fact, real, or rather represented a real god worthy of worship, then even the calf itself has cast Israel aside.

The other interpretation, obviously favored by almost all translators after Webster, follows the LXX, which has "you shall turn your calf, O Samaria," which apparently means that Samaria must cast away her calf because God already has.

Either interpretation works for the context, though apparently the weight of scholarship is with the modern choice: "Your calf-idol is rejected, Samaria" (CSB).

The application of such a charge is self-evident to the modern Christian: It is wise to make a good beginning in the faith and to clear out sinful practices and indulgences early. The foundations God's people lay determine the kind of house they build; and a house built on a swamp is likely to be filled with mildew and rot.

The reference to **innocency** is taken by some versions to mean "capable of purity," casting the Hebrew in the positive rather than the negative. Probably it does not mean that they were expected to "clean up their act" sufficiently to be regarded as innocent—which is not strictly biblical. Rather it means that being "cleansed" (Douay-Rheims) required them to put away their idols and confess all their sin before, or certainly as, they came to the Lord for purification and forgiveness. The question as asked, however, was rhetorical.

The **calf** was **from Israel**—"And this calf—it didn't fall out of heaven: you Israelites made it." Recall the passage in Exodus where the people demanded something visible, tangible, to worship since Moses had disappeared into Mt. Sinai and might even be dead. Aaron told them to bring their gold jewelry, and he made an idol for them. But his report to Moses was, "So they gave it me: then I cast it into the fire, and there came out this calf." One wonders if Aaron expected Moses to believe even partly that the calf emerged on its own. Here in Hosea, God's declaration that Israel made her calf is meant to counteract the notion that somehow the idol they worshiped revealed itself to the nation, or the nations around them that originally served the calf idol(s).

Compare with Jeremiah 10:3-5, where the prophet describes the craftsman's creation of an idol of wood, which manifestly cannot speak, or move, or bless anyone. The **calf of Samaria** will be shattered, and neither it nor any being represented by it would be able to prevent or even mitigate.

7   **For they have sown the wind, and they shall reap the whirlwind...**

Anything **sown** is expected to come up multiplied. This includes **wind,** which elsewhere in scripture suggests something vapid, insubstantial, even foolish (Job 7:7, Proverbs 11:29, Ecclesiastes 1:14). If Israel had sown faithfulness, loyalty to God, honor of the commandments, and the sole worship of Yahweh, they would be hearing his promises of blessing instead of his pronouncements of destruction. Instead, their lives had been invested in worthless things, and the return on this investment would be the vortex of the withdrawal of God's Spirit.

8   **Israel is swallowed up...**

Is is predictive. Presently it will happen. When Israel is conquered, captured, and carted off, it will be absorbed into the enemy's people and will not be reestablished.

...a vessel wherein is no pleasure.

Many translators take the **vessel** to be pottery, and if that's what Hosea's illustration meant, he must have implied that the vessel was broken. Why keep it if it is useless?

9 **For they are gone up to Assyria, a wild ass alone by himself: Ephraim hath hired lovers.**

The AV has "himself," translating the Hebrew *low* as "by **himself**) only to agree in gender with the proper name Ephraim yet to come. As previously noted, Hosea repeatedly uses the personal name of Ephraim to represent Israel (also a personal name, of course, but usually meant in Hosea's writing as a reference to the nation). In this particular image of a wild donkey, it does not trouble Hosea that the name is male and the donkey in heat is female. No doubt his readers got the point. The frequent image of Ephraim/Israel as a prostitute is a mixed metaphor. It was, as it still is, common to refer to nations with female pronouns and allusions. What was unusual was the idea that Israel *the prostitute* was paying for her lovers. The usual case is the other way around. What is implied is a measure of desperation. The donkey wanders around braying, trying to find a temporary mate. It was Ephraim, Israel, trading whatever it had for friendship and security in times that threatened war and defeat.

10 **Yea, though they have hired among the nations, now will I gather them, and they shall sorrow a little for the burden of the king of princes.**

Hired means Israel had sold themselves out. They made international deals that put them at the mercy of others. Though God would **gather** them, it would not be in Israel, but in the land of a conqueror, and he, the **king of princes,** would make life hard for them. The LXX rendered two words with a little alteration, resulting in something like, "and they shall stop for a while anointing kings and princes," i.e. they would no longer be in charge of their national affairs and destiny. The difference between the Septuagint's translation of the Hebrew and virtually any modern translation of the Masoretic text is quite dramatic, but interestingly enough both versions make sense in context.

11 Because Ephraim hath made many altars to sin, altars shall be unto him to sin.

Israel constructed many altars for the ostensible purpose of atoning for their sins—but altars not authorized by Yahweh. And through their conduct there at those altars they multiplied their sinful guilt. The altars were no doubt intended to offer multiple sites for worship of the LORD, which had been King Jeroboam's plan to keep the Israelites from feeling they had to go back into Judah to worship (1 Kings 12:31). For something tangible to attract their worship, Jeroboam had made two golden calves (1 Kings 12:28), proclaiming them an apt representation of the LORD that they could gather around, in lieu of the temple. Both things were part of Israel's current sinfulness, since the images were confused with Baal worship and the many altars continued to be disallowed substitutes for central worship in the temple.

12 I have written to him the great things of my law, but they were counted as a strange thing.

Written means not that God had given Israel separate or additional scriptures but that they were the original recipients, along with Judah and Benjamin, of the **Law**—the books of Moses. What characterized Israel's national sin so dramatically was its willing ignorance of that law and indeed its contempt for it. Most translations have **strange** where the KJV does, or "foreign," but we think the NLT's paraphrase is most accurate: "they act as if those laws don't apply to them."

13 **They sacrifice flesh for the sacrifices of mine offerings, and eat it; but the LORD accepteth them not…**

The verse is offered as if in counterpoint to an argument that might be offered by Israel—that it followed multiple commandments for offerings, etc. They sacrificed and had the holy meals. Hosea, speaking for the Lord, doesn't even argue with the assertion that these were **mine offerings** *(habhabay)*. But these were a formality (Amplified Bible). Because their hearts were not right and their lives were wildly sinful, the Lord did not accept their obedience to ritual.

…now will he remember their iniquity, and visit their sins: they shall return to Egypt.

Their figurative return **to Egypt** would be a fitting redress for their rejection of the devoted worship of the Lord and faithful living for him. Whenever the scriptures state that the Lord remembers something, it is a literary device to introduce a forthcoming action the Lord is about to take.

14 **For Israel hath forgotten his Maker, and buildeth temples…**

This summary sentence is really striking. Israel has abandoned the worship of God, his maker, the Almighty Lord, and in its place he has simply built edifices in which to conduct all manner of rituals and feasts and ungodly things.

Temples in the KJV translates the Hebrew *hekalowt*, which probably should be, as almost all other translations have it, "palaces." Used in the singular it appears dozens of times in the scriptures as a reference to the temple at Jerusalem. But its root words are not specific to worship but only to a "great house." However, it is undeniable that Hosea means it to represent the places where Israel worshiped instead of going to the temple.

...and Judah hath multiplied fenced cities: but I will send a fire upon his cities, and it shall devour the palaces thereof.

Turning to the southern kingdom for another, occasional warning, Hosea focuses not on any false worship but instead on their defensive build-up. **Fenced** is obviously "fortified" or "walled." Interestingly, Hosea here uses the specific word for "palaces" *(armənoteha)*. Both the fortifications and the sumptuous residences of kings and princes indicate the secular and political remedies Judah sought for her upcoming threats. Repeatedly Judah had chosen anything *but* trusting and obeying the Lord as the best defense.

This verse depicts the vacuousness of the worship of both the southern and northern kingdoms and the certainty of their punishment. No cruise missile will intercept God's judgment. No radar will even see it coming. When God begins his desert storm, his targets will be consumed.

As a matter of application, the reader may consider:

- The tendency of some nominal Christians to build churches mostly as monuments to men and places for them to practice their brand of self-assurance (v11).
- The statement of purporting Christians to believing in the Bible, but a demonstrable lack of the knowledge of it, or the practice of its precepts (v12).
- The occasional or even mostly regular attendance of nominal Christians to worship, followed by impure lives, tainted business dealings, and relationships without any semblance of Christian witness (v13a).

Chapter 9

To many if not most people whose context for life is biblical, a continuing mystery is God's not bringing judgment on the earth. He is obviously waiting for something. Periods of almost incredibly evil activity have taken place during history, times when Christians have predicted the events of the eschaton, and yet it has not happened. Times of intense persecution of godly people have convinced those being slain for their faith that the second-coming of Christ must be only hours away, but it wasn't. The inaction of God in this regard has been seen as curious and inexplicable at the very least.

However, equally curious would be the question of God's patience in bringing discipline on his people—whether Israel of old or the church today. Those who name the name of Christ are generally not eager to have their corporate or individual sins dealt with by the divine Judge, even though they know it is written: "For it is time for judgment to begin with God's household" (1 Peter 4: 17 NIV).

As Hosea listened to the word of the Lord coming into him and flowing out of him, he spoke of a time to come when Israel would finally reap what it had been sowing through the times of its rebel kings and through the eras of its imitation of the vile and corrupt nations around it. The few people in Israel who still were grieved and outraged by the wickedness of life around them probably wondered why the fire hadn't fallen yet. But it was about to. The complete punishment of Israel would come in its experience of human tragedy and finally enslavement.

1   **Rejoice not, O Israel, for joy, as other people: for thou hast gone a whoring from thy God, thou hast loved a reward upon every cornfloor.**

The meaning of the verse is quite plain. The question that poses itself is why other nations are not being rebuked for "rejoicing," which must be taken to mean the seasonal celebration of the countries around Israel, as they observed harvest festivals and the like. Why, if they held religious events honoring Baal and other gods, were they not being roundly condemned by Hosea? In point of fact, their sins were being noted and they would eventually be dealt with, but it was not *they* to whom the Law had come, not *they* who were called to be a "peculiar people" (Deuteronomy 14:2 *et al.*). Israel as a whole, both north and south, had been singled out among the nations to belong to the Lord and to receive the law and the covenants (cp. Deuteronomy 32:9, Romans 9:4). When they sinned nationally like other nations sinned continually, it was with even greater guilt. They had been unfaithful—**gone a whoring from thy God.**

Whether this charge was meant figuratively or literally is the relevant interpretive question in this verse and indeed in the entire chapter, as it has been all along in Hosea. And as before, it may not make a great deal of difference. If the charge is meant literally, that **thou hast loved a reward on every cornfloor,** then every reader or listener contemporary with Hosea would know he was condemning the wild and immoral carousing of people all over the country on the threshing floors, where after a day's work and the falling of night, prostitution at the threshing floor was rampant. If Hosea's language was intended to be taken more symbolically, then his condemnation extended to any national way of life that constituted spiritual unfaithfulness to God. The weakness of the entirely-literal view is that it would have applied to fewer people, while the symbolic view would indict the entire nation, which seems more the scope of Hosea's preaching and writing.

Yet, the literal view of **whoring** cannot be ignored, since the judgments that were to come upon Israel would be focused at least in part on the sites of her sinfulness:

2 **The floor and the winepress shall not feed them, and the new wine shall fail in her.**

The very threshing **floor** where prostitution for Baal was taking place would be targeted by God's hand of judgment, as crops would fail. And the **new wine** trodden out in the winepresses would not be abundant. The Hebrew *tirosh* here is almost always translated "new wine," of course. Why the new wine fails, however, is not due to any magical disappearance of the wine itself, but from the failure of the grape crops to begin with.

3   They shall not dwell in the LORD's land; but Ephraim shall return to Egypt, and they shall eat unclean things in Assyria.

    Egypt is partly figurative, while **Assyria** is literal. A few Israelites would anticipate Assyrian defeat and capture and flee to Egypt, thinking it secure; Israel had sought Egyptian help against Assyria and Egypt would take in some of their refugees. But as in 8:13, Egypt is also a symbol of captivity. Assyria, however, was the actual international threat, soon to be realized. And while Israel, as it was presently behaving, may not have been strictly attentive to its dietary laws, they would scarcely be able to obey them even if they wanted to, once forced into captivity. **Unclean things** is simply "unclean" *(tame)* and referred to anything the Jews were to consider unclean "to them."

4   They shall not offer wine offerings to the LORD, neither shall they be pleasing unto him...

    Wine offerings is simply "wine" in the Hebrew *(yayin)*. That "offerings" is meant is understood; however, as a follow-up thought to v2, it is apparent that they will not have an abundance of wine to begin with. The failure to make offerings of it may point either to the wine's scarcity or to the people's indifference.

...their sacrifices shall be unto them as the bread of mourners; all that eat thereof shall be polluted: for their bread for their soul shall not come into the house of the LORD.

    This prediction about the **bread of mourners** seems generally to be a reference to regulations about contact or even proximity to dead bodies, such as in Leviticus 21:1-5 and Ezekiel 44:25. The Lord was saying there was simply no way the Israelites would be able to be considered "clean," given their sinful state and the ongoing of God's judgment. Nothing they had was worthy to be offered in sacrifice, nor would it be.

5   **What will ye do in the solemn day, and in the day of the feast of the LORD?**

   Solemn is simply "appointed" —and so, most versions. There is a distinction made between the "appointed day(s)" and the "day of the feast of the Lord," but what difference it is isn't clear. If the cycle of feasts in the year were in view, perhaps the Feast of Trumpets or the Day of Atonement would be highlighted and referred to as the **feast of the Lord.** The point is well made even without certainty about which feasts are meant: when it would be most important for them to observe worship with solemnity and with the appropriate sacrifices, they wouldn't be able to do so.

6   **For, lo, they are gone because of destruction: Egypt shall gather them up, Memphis shall bury them: the pleasant places for their silver, nettles shall possess them: thorns shall be in their tabernacles.**

   Those who do flee to Egypt will not find hosts who coddle and celebrate them; they will simply absorb and then bury them. The image of their **silver** things being overtaken by **nettles** and their **tabernacles** (better, "tents") by thorns seems to suggest that their flight to Egypt will be sudden when they become convinced they have no alternative, and that things will be left behind—no time to organize, pack, and move lazily southward. What they leave is depicted as being overtaken by desert.

7   **The days of visitation are come, the days of recompence are come;**

Israel shall know it: the prophet is a fool, the spiritual man is mad, for the multitude of thine iniquity, and the great hatred.

The **visitation,** of course, is that of God in judgment, as in Isaiah 10:3). **Are come** is a declaration of the time period of the judgment, not the moment. And the closer the actual moment, the more the **spiritual man,** or the prophet, is considered by the vile, adulterous, idolatrous public to be insane, foolish.

Our present culture marginalizes men of God, comparing them unfairly to the true fools of the past who misused the word of God or set up churches as monuments to themselves. Every man or woman who roused up a community with predictions of the end of time will be used as ammunition to shoot down the preaching of faithful men of God who warn the culture of the **visitation** of God when it is truly imminent. But the culture's dismissal of the urgent warnings of God's messengers is not, and will not be, so much a thoughtful consideration of how many previous "prophets" have been wrong, as it will be because of **the multitude of thine iniquity.** People reject the message of sinful man's need of God and God's coming visitation of judgment because they have corrupt hearts. The heart of sinful man rejects God because he has **great hatred** of the holiness and righteousness of God. **Great hatred,** *(mastemah),* could be rendered simply "enmity." Among the Old Testament passages that declare the depravity of man this should be considered an important and useful one. It illustrates the necessity for an act of God in bringing about conviction of sin and a desire to repent. Without God's movement upon the heart, man will reject him out of enmity for the very one who created him.

This charge of foolishness is the source of perhaps the greatest temptation for the preacher of righteousness to alter or tone down his message. Yet it is exactly this "foolishness" that New Testament gospel proclaimers embrace (1 Corinthians 1:25). Those saved by grace know that the world's charge of the folly of "religious nonsense" is not a cogent or even logical argument or one backed up by sound evidence, but rather the response of the sin nature defending itself against divine invasion.

8   The watchman of Ephraim was with my God: but the prophet is a snare of a fowler in all his ways, and hatred in the house of his God.

This is another verse where the original is of uncertain meaning. The difficulty seems to come in the assumption of the verb "to be" where it was not intended. Even in the King James the prophet appears "to be" the fowler's snare, which is confusingly opposite of the expected sense. Construing the equivalencies another way, the paraphrased verse might read: "The watchman of Ephraim [i.e. the prophet], is God's man, but everywhere he goes he meets fowlers' snares, and even in God's house he is 'the enemy.'" The **snares** are the endless ways enemies of God's truth try to trap or trip up God's messengers.

9   They have deeply corrupted themselves, as in the days of Gibeah: therefore he will remember their iniquity, he will visit their sins.

The reference to Gibeah is to the story in Judges 19-20, where homosexual men of Gibeah, a city in the territory of Benjamin, first attempted to seize and rape a visiting Levite, but when thwarted, raped and killed his concubine instead. In the ensuing retribution carried out by the other tribes, the tribe of Benjamin was nearly wiped out. The entire episode was sordid and inextricably laced with a moral sickness that illustrated the deep depravity in Israel, even at such an early stage.

Hosea's comparison of Israel at present with its ancestors a few hundred years previous was intended to show that the present sins were no anomaly, but rather a deeply embedded trait of a morally wandering people.

Here again, God **remembers their iniquity,** meaning he is about to act—and indeed he will, when he **visits their sins.**

10 I found Israel like grapes in the wilderness; I saw your fathers as the firstripe in the fig tree at her first time…

This is God's musing, "Remember when?…" He looks back in their history to the time of his choice of Abraham, who bore Isaac, who bore Jacob—Israel—and he recalls the sense of promise that was there in those patriarchs. But those days are gone.

This is a good example of anthropomorphism, an expression of God's ways—who is not human—in terms of human emotions and thoughts. Hosea was unable, as are we all, of conceiving of God without some comparative reference to ourselves.

The comparison of Israel to **grapes in the wilderness** is meant to convey the sense of an exceptional find, a delight where it wasn't expected, where the **firstripe in the fig tree** is in an expected place but still presents a pleasant discovery for enjoyment. The Bible reader who looks back may not find in the history of the twelve sons of Jacob any remarkable sense of promise, but their potential did not consist of a merely human assessment of their accomplishments but instead of a divine plan for their heritage.

…but they went to Baalpeor, and separated themselves unto that shame; and their abominations were according as they loved.

According to Numbers 25, during the wilderness period the men of Israel were attracted to the women of Moab and a significant number of them involved themselves with these woman and subsequently the worship of Baal on Peor (**Baalpeor**), a mountain in Moab. This was a significant source of idolatrous infection that brought swift action from Moses. The reader of Numbers isn't told until 31:16, however, of the involvement of the seer Balaam in the affair. Balaam had been sought by Balak, king of Moab, to curse Israel, but he repeatedly blessed them because God wouldn't let him do otherwise. However, he subsequently advised the Moabites to use their women—especially the Baal prostitutes—to seduce Israelite men, which had a subversive effect on all of Israel.

This early involvement of Israel with Baal worship created a haunting legacy of idolatry that produced periodic, bitter fruit, ultimately culminating in the spiritual dissipation of the nation during Hosea's time, and the end of the northern and then the southern kingdoms.

The final verses of chapter 9 seem like a reversal of Genesis 1:28. God strikes at the very reproductive hopes of Israel:

11 As for Ephraim, their glory shall fly away like a bird, from the birth, and from the womb, and from the conception.

Ephraim/Israel will watch their national hopes fly away swiftly like a bird. The order of **birth, womb** and **conception** is backwards from how these things proceed in life. The sense is: You will see nothing born, because nothing is in the womb, because nothing was conceived. Their expectation of national deliverance and glory was being erased backwards, as if there had never been any promise to begin with.

12 Though they bring up their children, yet will I bereave them, that there shall not be a man left: yea, woe also to them when I depart from them!

The sweeping removal of Israel's future depicted in v11 is followed by what looks like an exception in v12, where some children indeed are born. The linguistic device is similar to that employed by the prophet Joel in 1:4: "What the locust swarm has left the great locusts have eaten; what the great locusts have left the young locusts have eaten; what the young locusts have left other locusts have eaten." The judgment comes in waves, the first nearly unexceptional, with the next and the next mopping up the remainder.

But the most awful prospect is not the punishments, but the fact that the Lord **departs from them.** For God to be present in discipline, as terrible as that can be, is less horrifying and dreadful than for him to be absent. To apply this principle on the grandest scale, this phrase in v12 is an apt description of the real horror of hell: it is a place and state from which God has entirely withdrawn his presence with all its redeeming influence.

13 Ephraim, as I saw Tyrus, is planted in a pleasant place: but Ephraim shall bring forth his children to the murderer.

The Lord, through Hosea, compares Ephraim/Israel to Tyre, the fantastic city on a rock in the Mediterranean out from a point in Lebanon. Ezekiel 27 is a chapter-long description of the beauty, richness and glory of this port city (of which Ezekiel prophesied the coming end). God compared his development and blessing of Israel in its northern region to the beauty of Tyre. But Israel had forfeited its future in God's continued blessing by its monumental sin. Its children would be "brought out" to **the murderer.** The depiction is a bit uncertain. The Hebrew *horeg* indeed means murderer or killer; the CSB's rendering of "executioner" is therefore a matter of inference. But exactly what Hosea had in mind as he envisioned what God was saying to him, we don't know. The general effect is not in question, however: the children, who are the future of any country, were not going to survive, and so the nation itself was going to perish.

14 Give them, O LORD: what wilt thou give? give them a miscarrying womb and dry breasts.

As most versions have it, the KJV's colon should be the modern "—". Hosea was searching for the right prophecy to be delivered. In the same vein as his prediction about Israel's children, he solemnly asks God to afflict Israel with miscarriages and the inability to nurse babies that actually are born.

While it could be surmised that this request of Hosea's was to mitigate the more severe prediction of the previous verse, the net effect would be the same: Israel's children would die.

15 All their wickedness is in Gilgal: for there I hated them…

For **Gilgal,** see above on 4:15. The mere mention of Gilgal was expected to bring up thoughts of the idolatry of which that place was a national center.

That God **hated them** at Gilgal should not be a disturbing thought. The popular notion of love and hate as emotions, while not antithetical to the Bible's description of God, are not the primary implications of these words. We are confronted with God's love and hate in the persons of Jacob and Esau, between whom God chose in the matter of his blessing and calling. Malachi later characterized the difference in this way: "Was not Esau Jacob's brother?" declares the LORD. "Yet Jacob I have loved, but Esau I have hated" (Malachi 1:2-3). But the revealing term in that passage is found in the first phrase of v2: "'I have loved you,' says the LORD. But you ask, '*How* have you loved us?'" Therein lies the emphasis in the definition of God's love. It is not simply an emotion he feels; it is an action he takes. God's choice to love Jacob was a choice to act toward Jacob and his descendants in a way different from his actions toward Esau—radically different.

Those who find a contradiction between statements that God "hates" something and the general truth expressed well by the Apostle John— "God is love" (1 John 4:16) should rather consider the more difficult challenge to our thought: how could God love anyone in this rebellious world, corrupted by sin?

That God **hated them** at Gilgal is as much, if not much more, an indication that his *actions* toward Israel took a turn toward their exclusion from his **house,** an expression for his withdrawing fellowship from them.

…for the wickedness of their doings I will drive them out of mine house, I will love them no more: all their princes are revolters.

God would **love them no more** in that he would turn away from them and reject them—*actions* that brought about their deserved destruction.

Are revolters is better "are rebellious" *(sorərim),* as in NIV, CSV, etc.

16 **Ephraim is smitten, their root is dried up, they shall bear no fruit: yea, though they bring forth, yet will I slay even the beloved fruit of their womb.**

The same linguistic device is used here as in v12. 'They won't have any children, and if they *do,* those children won't survive.'

17 **My God will cast them away, because they did not hearken unto him: and they shall be wanderers among the nations.**

The striking thing about this prophetic prediction is that Israel would not simply be defeated and taken captive, but that it would be dispersed **among the nations** where it (they) would **wander.** Much later, Titus of Rome destroyed Jerusalem in A.D. 70, resulting in the diaspora, a dispersion of Jews into the whole known world. This dispersion was certainly well described as "wandering among the nations," but the immediate event to Hosea would be the dispersion of the northern kingdom, which essentially dissolved into the peoples of Assyria and Babylon. When some return to the "promised land" took place, inaugurating the "second-temple period," it was chiefly the southern tribes who could be identified.

Infertility, miscarriage, stillbirths, crib death, infant epidemics, childhood diseases, malnutrition, all are possible tools of cutting off the literal, biological fruitfulness of a sinning nation. All these things were predicted—and soon to take place—for the northern kingdom. There would be no Israel/Ephraim anymore. The death of a nation itself would seem to be sufficient punishment for the enormity of its sins.

Excursus on God's Justice

A seemingly endless list of punishments pronounced on Israel, or on any other nation for that matter, begins to depress the average Bible reader eventually, and to tempt him to raise the question of the justice of God. Surely, the reader might think, this piling-on of punishments constitutes overkill. Does it?

The main reasons human beings question the justice of God when contemplating such severe punishment—and especially with regard to the dire warnings of the biblical hell—are three:

(1) We have short memories with great editing facilities;

(2) We have little concept of the holiness of God and his hatred of sin; and

(3) We fail to realize that a Sovereign God can do anything he likes with his universe, and it is right, when he does it, by definition.

Especially where the "innocent" suffer with the guilty (cp. Genesis 18:25), the Bible reader may still be left feeling resentful, but he must answer the question that emerges from that thought: Who is *innocent?*

The bottom line, while it will not satisfy the defensive objections of non-believers and may leave even believers with nagging questions and mixed feelings, is this: our meager perspectives are wholly insufficient to understand God's holiness and righteousness, and we are in no way qualified to advise him.

Chapter 10

Internal woes, disease, and economic disasters are not all God uses to judge sinful nations. Usually there are political instruments as well. A nation, like an individual, may conceive of a sense of its purpose and place in the divine scheme. Especially when that nation is linked through its origins and internal character to the mission of God in the world, it will eventually realize that God holds it to a higher standard than other nations. And its people, many of them, will realize that the specter of their national dissolution, even their overthrow, is a message from God about their utter depravity.

This description applies to Israel, but it has similar applications to any nation blessed through the providence of God with the opportunity in history to be the breeding ground of truth and righteousness. When the godly purpose of such a nation is abandoned, a virtual doomsday plan goes into effect.

1   **Israel is an empty vine, he bringeth forth fruit unto himself: according to the multitude of his fruit he hath increased the altars; according to the goodness of his land they have made goodly images.**

The curious problem in this verse is with the Hebrew *boqeq,* translated **empty** in the KJV. The word appears in Isaiah 24:1 where the KJV translates it the same way. However, if taken in the negative sense where to be empty is to be devoid of fruit, it conflicts with the next phrase. The translators of the Septuagint apparently had access to other texts, for they rendered the word as ευκληματουσα (*euklamatousa),* which means luxuriant or lush. Even in modern Greek the word means hardy. It is possible to keep the KJV's rendering *if* the interpretation is that the vine empties itself of its lush fruit. But that is probably unnecessary if the sources for the LXX were correct.

If the above interpretation is accurate, the condemnation of the verse lies in the fact that although Israel had experienced abundant harvests, they had used their agricultural enrichment to fund the creation of even more altars and images of Baals to worship.

An alternate reading of the verse might support the King James's choice of words, which after all have support in the Masoretic text and the passage in Isaiah. It is possible to read the first phrase as an indictment of Israel *itself* as an empty—fruitless—vine, while the rest of the verse speaks to the reason for such a condition: they had received the blessing of God on their harvests and had used their economic growth to enhance the worship of all gods other than the LORD.

2   **Their heart is divided; now shall they be found faulty: he shall break down their altars, he shall spoil their images.**

The key word in this verse, *halaq,* translated **divided**, is usually rendered as "allotted" or "divided." But modern translators are all over the place in rendering it in this context: deceitful, fickle, false, devious, faithless, disloyal, and slipping, are some of the translations. In view of the frequent meaning of "divided," where allotment of land was being described, it does not seem problematic to stick with "divided," and it has the support of the LXX. Few readers would fail to understand that a divided heart means one that professes devotion to two or more persons—or gods, in this context—and that the ones to whom they claim to be loyal have competing and conflicting demands. In this case, Yahweh demanded exclusive loyalty, and Baals and other gods were siphoning off Israel's attentions.

To the extent that Israel gave *any* loyalty at all to *any* other god, it was being rebellious against Yahweh, and on that basis alone it was **faulty** *(yesamu)*. The Psalmist uses this word in 34:21 to mean "desolate." The people who emptily pledge belief in the God of All will find themselves suddenly without God at all.

3   **For now they shall say, We have no king, because we feared not the LORD; what then should a king do to us?**

The connecting thoughts between the three parts of this verse are unclear from the Hebrew. It appears to mean: "People will wonder if they have no king because they didn't fear the Lord. But even if they did have a king, what could he do to remedy the situation of impending doom?" Hosea watched a succession of short-lived kings try to take control of a country careening down a path to being conquered and overrun.

4 **They have spoken words, swearing falsely in making a covenant: thus judgment springeth up as hemlock in the furrows of the field.**

Translators of the NIV and CSV found in the Hebrew *mispat* (**judgment**) the suggestion of "lawsuit," and so rendered it. The somewhat obscure original produces conflicting interpretations by way of translation. For instance, *berit,* rendered "covenant" here, may mean oath, agreement, treaty, or contract, and various translators have used those words in the plural though the Hebrew is singular. It isn't likely that if the word means "covenant" it refers to the covenant with God. Likely it refers to human contracts.

Perhaps the sense of the verse is that there was such widespread dishonesty and falsity that everything from business dealings to family life to government was awash in false promises and uncertainty, resulting in widespread injustice and cheating.

5 **The inhabitants of Samaria shall fear because of the calves of Bethaven: for the people thereof shall mourn over it, and the priests thereof that rejoiced on it, for the glory thereof, because it is departed from it.**

On **Bethaven** see on 4:15. This verse is another whose elements are connected in some implicit way not agreed upon by modern translators. The **calves** of Bethaven should be singular as it is in the Hebrew. The golden calf worshiped at the high place of Bethaven was greatly revered. Remember that the golden calf had a relatively long history in Israel's worship. Those who became ecstatic in the worship that centered or focused on it were going to be deathly afraid that whatever supernatural being inhabited the calf would wreak havoc with them for its being carted off to Assyria (**departed**).

6   **It shall be also carried unto Assyria for a present to king Jareb: Ephraim shall receive shame, and Israel shall be ashamed of his own counsel.**

See above on 5:13 for a discussion of **king Jareb.** The fruit of all Israel's attempts to stave off invasion and absorption will be shame for its failures and useless treaties.

7   **As for Samaria, her king is cut off as the foam upon the water.**

If we accept the King James's word "foam," we may assume that Hosea used the image of foam on water, perhaps from a waterfall into a muddy pond, drifting downstream and popping, bubble by bubble, until they are all gone, subsumed into the rushing current. The line of Israel's kings will disappear, faster and faster, until no successors remain and no kingdom remains to reign over. The enemy has **cut** them **off.**

But the Hebrew has "twig" for what the KJV renders "foam," as does the LXX (φρυγανον - *phruganon*). A twig may float downstream once it has been **cut off** from a tree above, but its disappearance would have to complete the image.

The point is that what is floating, carried along on the water, is not in charge, but is at the mercy of the flow, until sucked under and buried with all the other detritus.

8   **The high places also of Aven, the sin of Israel, shall be destroyed...**

The **high places** were the quintessence of Israel's sin, having been used by Canaanite worshipers before the land was even conquered under Joshua, and having been revived in the northern kingdom for the professed worship of the Lord, though specifically condemned as such.

They were centers of immoral revelry and bastardized worship. And they were strongholds of demonic influence; the few kings who attempted to remove them had been unable to do so completely. They always came back, because the deep, idolatrous infection of the people was never cured. These places would be destroyed, even though that destruction would not be by a conqueror who intended to worship the true God.

…the thorn and the thistle shall come up on their altars; and they shall say to the mountains, Cover us; and to the hills, Fall on us.

The rubble of the structures and altars on the high places would be overgrown and overrun with **thorn and thistle**, and **they shall say—** Who shall say, "**Fall on us**"? Most translations leave it to the reader to conclude whether the previously mentioned "Israel" is the speaker, through its remaining people, or whether Hosea is using a poetic device, personifying the rubble. Given that the high places are by definition *high,* no mountains could fall on them. We prefer to think that "people" is the understood subject—people who, left behind, are immersed in shame and wish their lives to end.

9 **O Israel, thou hast sinned from the days of Gibeah: there they stood: the battle in Gibeah against the children of iniquity did not overtake them.**

On **Gibeah**, see 9:9 and a description of the sin of the Benjamites. While in an immediate sense, as Hosea implies, Israel punished the Benjamites justly, in the larger sense Israel indulged in a kind of murderous overkill that wiped out "righteous" with wicked. And in no sense did the vile, sinful hearts that infested not only Benjamin but all the tribes, by that point, go away. It came under some degree of control in the united kingdom but festered and then exploded when the kingdoms separated.

This was Hosea's point: that Israel had continued to sin since the

days of Gibeah, and in the same ways. And appropriately, it would be at Gibeah (as well as other key places of idolatry and licentiousness) that Israel would itself finally be punished.

10 It is in my desire that I should chastise them...

The KJV supplies "It is," where other versions assume something like "when." CSV has "at my discretion," which is certainly the sense of the Hebrew *bɔawwati.* **Chastise,** or discipline, is distinguished from "punish," in that it leaves room for the repentance and reconciliation that discipline is designed to bring about. And though such a future has not been much in view throughout Hosea, the upcoming echo of v12 will sound that note again, as though there were a remote chance that a very few of Israel had a brief window of opportunity to escape irremediable judgment.

...and the people shall be gathered against them, when they shall bind themselves in their two furrows.

The picture of this verse is that God will bind them (the Hebrew says, "*when* I bind them") and **people** (foreign powers) will be God's instrument of discipline, because of Israel's **two** sins. The two **furrows** Israel has plowed for herself (see v13), planting the seeds of her own destruction, are her rejection of God and her embrace of idol worship.

11 And Ephraim is as an heifer that is taught, and loveth to tread out the corn; but I passed over upon her fair neck: I will make Ephraim to ride; Judah shall plow, and Jacob shall break his clods.

Heifers were trained to work the threshing floor, going round and round in the grain and able to eat to their content. But God was going to subject Israel to a yoke, which would wear and chafe on that **fair neck,** and Judah would be right behind her.

The description of this plowing follows the previous image of

Israel's having sown the seeds of her own judgment. The specific symbolism of v11 is unclear, but it sets up the thought of v12. In the hard labor of the times that are coming, what should Israel do? Should it abandon hope and sow even more wickedness in a land where the worship of the Lord was not taught or followed? Or should Ephraim proceed as directed by v12:

12 **Sow to yourselves in righteousness, reap in mercy; break up your fallow ground: for it is time to seek the LORD, till he come and rain righteousness upon you.**

Israel should **sow** obedience to God's word, which will result in God's blessing them with his faithful love (**mercy**). They should address things in their individual lives and their lives as a people that have been unattended to for generations (**fallow ground**). Surely these included the reestablishment of worship as commanded long ago, and a revival of biblical morality. Their family lives had to be brought into order so as to support the teaching of godly values laid out in the Law. The function of the priesthood had to be recovered, building again as if from the beginning on the texts of the Torah. And in all this they were to **seek the Lord** on a personal and community level, in humility and repentance and earnest petition, until he answered them and showered them with good things again (**rain righteousness**).

13 **Ye have plowed wickedness, ye have reaped iniquity; ye have eaten the fruit of lies: because thou didst trust in thy way, in the multitude of thy mighty men.**

The momentary glimpse of hopeful thought in v12 is put aside again for a recap of what Israel has done, leading up to this point. It is expressed in the same agricultural idiom. They had sown wicked living and reaped **iniquity**. The Hebrew generally means wicked deeds, but some translators take the word *awlatah* to mean calamitous results, or generally bad things, much in the same way as people speak of "natural evils" referring to earthquakes, tornados and the like. The Amplified Bible takes the word to imply the injustice or evil wreaked on Israel by others. Some other versions have "perversity." The point is that nothing good came of their wicked living, but instead everything bad.

The spiritual root of this wicked living was the failure—indeed the refusal—to **trust** God, and instead the inclination to put their stock in political strength and military might. While the dread of the Israelite armies once prompted surrender or sincerely-sought treaties (e.g. Joshua 9:3-27), those days were gone.

14 Therefore shall a tumult arise among thy people, and all thy fortresses shall be spoiled, as Shalman spoiled Betharbel in the day of battle: the mother was dashed in pieces upon her children.

Most authorities think **Shalman** here was Shalmaneser (2 Kings 17:3), the king of Assyria. It isn't necessary to have a confirming description from some other source to understand that Hosea was calling on the remembrance of the Israelites that a place called Betharbel was violently destroyed by Shalmaneser. The Israelites' recollection of the gruesome reports of atrocities perpetrated on **mother**s and their **children** was enough to make the point that the days ahead for Israel itself were to be feared.

25 So shall Bethel do unto you because of your great wickedness: in a morning shall the king of Israel utterly be cut off.

The LXX has an opposite take on the sense of the verse. The Hebrew appears to be correct, if for no other reason than its consistency with the previous verse and the whole chapter in general. Just as "Beth-arbel's" destruction was an example of prior Assyrian conquest, so in Israel's near future "Beth-el's" conquest loomed. And it would not take long, when Assyria swept in for the kill. "At dawn" *(bassahar)* Israel's king would be cut off. That king would be Hoshea, who reigned about ten years.

The tone of previous chapters has been overwhelmingly negative, in wave after wave of indictments and judgments. Beginning with chapter 11, Hosea speaks God's word with its mingling of wistful remembrance, sad conclusions and ardent grief.

Chapter 11

If one takes a view of the process of prophecy in the mind and heart of the prophet like the one we take in this commentary, the prophet was inspired by the profound thoughts and powerful feelings he experienced as he viewed and analyzed the situation of the country before him. While many of the prophets had visionary encounters with the Lord that went beyond merely the deep devotion of other holy people, we are convinced most of their vocalization of what God was saying to them was not the repetition of dictated words. Rather their prophecies were their sure expression of convictions of which they had absolutely no doubt, and predictions of tomorrow that were as certain to them as their remembrances of yesterday.

During the ministry of Hosea things looked bleak for Israel. Hosea realized that at his moment in history, very shortly God would bring Assyria against the northern kingdom and virtually wipe her from existence. But he also sensed the glimmer of hope that existed in the mysterious, ancient love of God that emanated from his inexplicable grace. For while the predictions for Israel that the Lord transmitted to Hosea were the dark color of wrath, that was not the only thing God "felt" concerning his chosen people. In the upcoming chapter and beyond, Hosea voices God's mixture of affection, disappointment and displeasure in the familiar tones of a father.

1 **When Israel was a child, then I loved him, and called my son out of Egypt.**

Hosea envisions **Israel** here as Jacob, whom God **loved** when he called him instead of his brother Esau. Skipping ahead through the lives of Jacob/Israel's sons, their move to Goshen during widespread famine, and four hundred years of increasing oppression and finally slavery, Hosea voices God's prophetic act: I **called my son out of Egypt.** This is a very direct and accurate assessment of what God did in the exodus of the Hebrew people from bondage under Pharaoh.

It is also an inscription on history that was invested with a predictive meaning, as the gospel writer Matthew realized, telling his readers that this verse was fulfilled in the Holy Spirit's directive to Joseph to take his family back to Israel from Egypt, where they had fled to avoid the infanticide of Herod. In returning and settling in Nazareth, he was bringing the Eternal Son Incarnate out of Egypt and back to the land where he would provide God's redemption from sin.

After this statement about Egypt, however, the balance of chapter 11 has no particular predictive significance for the Messiah who was to come.

In a proper perspective on the prescience of prophecy, it should not be difficult to accept the occasional predictive nature of a striking statement in the midst of narrative that may not otherwise prompt the reader to think of a future personage or future events. For instance, the sign Isaiah gave king Ahaz in Isaiah 7:14 stood out as an unusual statement—debatable even then as to its degree of possibility—that a virgin (Hebrew *almah* - "young woman") would conceive and bear a son and call him Immanuel. But the description of the following events then began immediately to reflect Isaiah and Ahaz's present historical context: Isaiah and his wife soon had a child whom they named Maher-Shalal-Hash-Baz, the description of whose childhood reflects the earlier prediction of 7:14.

Similarly, here in Hosea 11:1 the prophet's short, declarative statement that God called his son out of Egypt stands out like a subject heading for the following material, which in turn describes the story of this son, Israel. The heading alone is invested with the prophecy that found fulfillment in the coming of God the Son to earth. There are no other parallels to Christ in the chapter.

2   As they called them, so they went from them: they sacrificed unto Baalim, and burned incense to graven images.

The Masoretic text has **they called,** etc, but the LXX has "As I called," which makes logical sense of the verse. God called Israel to

himself, but they went away from him and sacrificed unto **Baalim** (the
Baal images). This compression of history is the bottom line of what
happened, of course, but understanding what took place over time is
important:

- Over several generations,
- through a series of political administrations,
- led by kings who were often evil or perverse,
- distanced from authentic priestly ministry,
- misled by the priests they had,
- lacking the knowledge of the written word of God of their time,
- and subjected to the longstanding influence of Canaanite religions that were never purged from Israelite territory,
- The Israelites lost their devotion as a people to the Lord and mirrored the religious beliefs and practices of the idolatrous world around them.

It is worth noting that this is precisely what Joshua predicted would
take place. Joshua reminded the Israelites that numbers of people of the
nations they were supposed to displace *remained among them* (Joshua 23:7)
and that the Israelites were not to serve those people's gods or invoke
their names. He told them they were not to ally themselves with the
survivors of those nations, not to intermarry with them, not even to
associate with them (Joshua 23:12). If they did, those people and their
religions "shall be snares and traps unto you, and scourges in your sides,
and thorns in your eyes, until ye perish from off this good land which
the LORD your God hath given you" (Joshua 23:13).

**3   I taught Ephraim also to go, taking them by their arms; but they
knew not that I healed them.**

Modern translations are divided about evenly on whether the image
is of the Lord's taking Ephraim **by** his arms to help him walk or *in* his

arms after his daring, infant steps. It hardly matters. The Greek of the LXX has επι *(epi)*, suggesting more the sense of "upon" or "in." The picture is, in any event, one of an affectionate father with his infant child, teaching him to walk.

What is symbolized is God's teaching Israel the Lord's ways as opposed to the ways of the peoples around him. Abraham had come out of Ur, his father still a worshiper of the various regional gods, unaware of the uniqueness of Yahweh. Abraham's son and grandson were surrounded by worshipers of regional deities. Jacob married Rachel, daughter of Laban, who had household gods, idols that Rachel purloined when she and Jacob were leaving to go to Gilead. Jacob's brother flouted the chosen monotheism of their father and grandfather by uniting himself with Mahalath, a Canaanite woman whose family no doubt worshiped numerous Baals. Without the Mosaic books and their record of the law for several hundred more years, the family of Abraham was guided by the Heavenly Father through the several theophanic appearances of Yahweh and the teaching of their patriarchs.

After the exodus and the giving of the law, Ephraim—along with the entire family of Jacob/Israel—was 'taught to walk' by training in the law, which incorporated the acceptable worship of God, the entire moral expectation of God, and the peculiar practices he wanted to identify his special people in the world. That the moral and ethical law of God dramatically differed from the peoples around Israel was patently obvious. What God the Father did was teach Ephraim to walk in a truly godly manner among the many perverse and demonic ways that stood out among Canaanites, Assyrians, Egyptians and other peoples.

The second phrase of v3 is something of a *non sequitur,* unless the image of the first implies that as the child of the illustration began to learn to walk he also fell and scraped his hands or knees. Then, the thought that the father **healed** him would follow logically. Again, it little matters. Children are typically unaware of the innumerable ways their parents solve the problems they create, care for the needs they have, and fix the things they break. Ephraim was essentially unaware of the great depths of grace and mercy to which the Lord went to forgive and restore them, until it was finally time to subject them to overwhelming discipline.

4 I drew them with cords of a man, with bands of love...

Several versions take the Hebrew *adam* here, which elsewhere ubiquitously means simply "man," to mean "affection" or "human kindness" (NIV). The LXX is confusing, with its reading, εν διαφθορα ανθροπων ("in corruption of men"). We think the modern translations are on the right track. God used means that translated into the equivalencies of human kindness and the attraction of love to convince Israel to be faithful to him.

...and I was to them as they that take off the yoke on their jaws, and I laid meat unto them.

The English is odd because the Hebrew is. It apparently contains idioms that shortly became obscure. The NIV ignores **yoke**, the literal meaning of the Hebrew *ol*, and interprets the phrase as meaning the father lifts the child to his cheek. The New KJV has "neck" for the older KJV's "jaws" —a plausible generalization of the Hebrew "*ləhehem.*" Most versions have some variation on 'lift the yoke from their jaws,' letting the reader deduce the fairly obvious meaning—though why a small child would have a yoke on his neck in the first place is not explained. However, this reasoning probably explains the NIV's consistency with the illustration.

Laid meat unto them is grossly archaic and simply means "bent down to feed them."

5 He shall not return into the land of Egypt, but the Assyrian shall be his king, because they refused to return.

Israel/Ephraim will not go back into bondage to Egypt (though a few people would flee there prior to the upcoming invasion—see above on 9:6); instead they will be captured by Assyria, because they refused to repent.

Some versions take the Hebrew to imply a rhetorical question demanding the understanding that Israel *will* return to Egypt. We think that the CSB's and others' conclusion is correct that Egypt is essentially out of the picture.

6   **And the sword shall abide on his cities, and shall consume his branches, and devour them, because of their own counsels.**

The **sword** is the divine judgment, the **cities** are just that, and the **branches** are the suburbs and towns on the roads that come from the cities. In other words, the hand of the Lord will be against the entire land, from the densest cores of their cities to the least populated outlying village, because of their **counsels**. The Hebrew word is used numerous other places, such as Psalm 81:12, where the writer says, "So I gave them up unto their own hearts' lust: and they walked in their own counsels." The idea of the word is that the Israelites did not seek the Lord's wisdom, the Lord's guidance, or the Lord's truth.

7   **And my people are bent to backsliding from me: though they called them to the most High, none at all would exalt him.**

The older translations mostly take the last phrase to say that Israel would not exalt God, while newer versions understand the original to say God would not exalt (i.e. pardon) Israel. The contrast and discrepancy are due to the inference of "him" in the final verb, *yərowmem*. To read the verb as implying "him" referring to God, the verse would require a change of voice in the middle, as if God spoke 7a but Hosea spoke 7b. We think the same voice makes more sense: "My people are bent on turning from me; and though they call to the Most High, they won't at all exalt him." These are a people who maintain a form of prayer, but it is without true praise and genuine worship.

8   How shall I give thee up, Ephraim? how shall I deliver thee, Israel? how shall I make thee as Admah? how shall I set thee as Zeboim? ...

The reader should imagine a pause between v7 and v8, as the prophet senses that God is turning another side of himself toward both prophet and people. Every prophet, like every human being, knows the capacity to exhibit anger righteously and yet feel the mitigating grace of love. The mixture of these things in the heart defines the idea of grief. It is natural for us, then, to conceive of God's deep grief, since he has indeed expressed himself toward us with both discipline and affection.

The Hebrew for "shall I give thee up," *ettenka,* is precisely the same as for "shall I make thee." In Ezekiel 35:9 the word is also translated "make." The Hebrew root has similar power to the French verb "faire" (to make or do) which it means, or even the English verb "do." Its meaning is understood by the words coming after it.

How could God give up Israel, turning it over to the Assyrians— much less make it like **Admah** or **Zeboim**? Admah and Zeboim were near Sodom and Gomorrah and suffered the same fate in the days of Lot (Deuteronomy 29:23). To speak of Admah and Zeboim was to speak of subjection to divine judgment.

...mine heart is turned within me, my repentings are kindled together.

The word *leb* (**heart**) further identifies this description of God as an unapologetically anthropomorphic one. That God at this point has "repentings" is troublesome to those who do not understand the necessities of a human description of the divine mind. The Hebrew can be translated "sympathies" (and has been), though its principle meaning is "turning." One should read that God is "changing his mind" but at the same time understand that the entire process of his articulation of wrath has been deliberately part of his revealing his grief—the admixture of anger and love. With this perspective, God's "repentance" can be understood. See the upcoming excursus on God's Repentance.

9   I will not execute the fierceness of mine anger, I will not return to destroy Ephraim...

Quite obviously, God did not decide to do *nothing* to Ephraim, but instead to stay his hand from the worst outcome. The **fierceness** of God's anger must be understood to be something so far beyond what he actually did in Israel's history as to be startling and utterly terrifying to contemplate.

...for I am God, and not man...

The irony of this phrase, literarily, is that Hosea has been writing with virtually blatant anthropomorphism, yet he understands God to be revealing himself as the farthest thing from human in his being. Specifically, what differs here is that God does not lose his temper, does not "shoot from the hip," and does not ever overreact. What he will do with regard to Ephraim will be measured, appropriate, fully justified, and completely righteous.

...the Holy One in the midst of thee...

This precise rendering of the original depicts God among and at the center of the nation—surely the expression of the ideal, as God intended things to be from the beginning with his people. It emphasizes the Lord's being a part *of* the people, not a deity apart *from* them.

...and I will not enter into the city.

Again, there may be a lost idiom in the final words, **enter into the city.** Most modern translators see the implication of destruction or wrath in the phrase and leave out the word "city" from their renderings. Keep in mind that earthly kings and armies of the time—indeed of all times—focused their attacks on cities, where after all the people and governments and commerce were.

10 **They shall walk after the LORD: he shall roar like a lion: when he shall roar, then the children shall tremble from the west.**

Building upon the preferred desire of the Lord's heart to spare Israel, Hosea writes of a time in the future when Israel would **walk after the LORD,** meaning to live with and for him faithfully. God is pictured here as a **lion,** which implies his warning to enemies. The lion leads the people protectively. **The west** *(miyam)* suggests Egypt, which the next verse would confirm, though it may refer to islands or lands to the west and northwest. The Douay -Rheims Bible, whose sources are the Vulgate and the Hebrew texts behind it, has "children of the sea."

The children implies "his," the Lord's, not some unidentified children. This term, instead of "Ephraim" or even "Israel," emphasizes the attitude that will be found in those who then **walk after the LORD:** They will return to God for forgiveness and restoration, and with an attitude of humility and reverence, as well as with eagerness and simplicity. Their hard service and subsequent relief will convince them God does not brook sin, but he does not stop loving them, either.

11 **They shall tremble as a bird out of Egypt, and as a dove out of the land of Assyria: and I will place them in their houses, saith the LORD.**

To the compass directions in v10, v11 adds the south and southwest in the nation of **Egypt,** and the east and northeast in the mention of **Assyria.** All the countries and areas now designated are the places that Israelites will be found when, after a time of dispersion, they are gathered again into the homeland God selected for them and promised them would be theirs. When they gather from all over the world, they will once again have **their houses,** their secure homes.

12 **Ephraim compasseth me about with lies, and the house of Israel with deceit: but Judah yet ruleth with God, and is faithful with the saints.**

This verse really belongs with chapter 12; its tone is again accusatory against Israel while at least partly affirming Judah, and these are the subject of chapter 12.

The **lies** of Ephraim are their claims to worship the Lord while they are active in serving Baal.

Modern translations are about evenly divided in their interpretation of what **Judah yet ruleth with God** means. The Hebrew seems to say, "but Judah still walks with God," while the LXX has something entirely different, including Judah with Ephraim's sins. If the balance of chapter 12 were used to interpret this verse, it would comport with the Septuagint. However, if one considers Hosea 1:7 and 4:15, this verse may indicate that God is noting Judah's not being as deeply entrenched in idolatry as his northern brother, which would help explain the generation of delay before Judah's being conquered, and the fact that when the tribes returned, it was Judah (and Benjamin) that dominated.

Excursus on God's Repentance

In the prophets and elsewhere in the Old Testament the reader is presented with the puzzling subject of God's repentance—his decision not to do something he planned to do. The mention of such a decision in Hosea 11:9 is one of the more explicit.

When the idea of repenting is connected to God, it must not be taken to mean that God is indecisive, or that he temporarily lost his temper and then got control of himself, or that he in any way acts like human beings do when they mis-speak or misbehave in the heat of passion.

In the passage in Hosea, God's own judgment of Israel was that they were perversely consumed by various passions, fully justifying the worst possible punishment. But in 11:9 he specifically disavows being a man or like a man in his response to human rebellion (or in any other way). He is "Holy," which in this context doubly indicates the idea of "other-ness," or difference.

But *can* God change his mind? What about passages such as Genesis 6:5-6, which speaks of God's repenting that he made man, of his attitude changing, and of his determining to alter his previous plans toward man? Many people believe, based on passages such as these and on Abraham's plea for Sodom—which elicited concessions from the Angel of the Lord— that God can be persuaded to change his mind. If so, not only does that conclusion seem to conflict with Malachi 3:6— "I am the Lord; I change not" —it raises the question about the propriety of his initial plans, in light of his altered ones. Several answers need to be given:

(1) Nothing God plans to do is ever anything but righteous. By definition, God's actions are right. There is no higher definition of righteousness by which God himself is evaluated.

(2) God's change of course is not the result of indecision or

fluctuating emotions. "The Strength of Israel will not lie nor repent: for he is not a man, that he should repent" (1 Samuel 15:29).

(3) God's altered actions are the demonstration of his possession of both wrath and mercy, and his judicious mixture of the two. He does this for our sakes, that we might constantly be reminded of both realities.

(4) God's plans often include both an action prompted by his justice and one inspired by his mercy; and he invites us to participate in his will by intercession. The parent who offers a choice of disciplines to his children is imitating God. God's plans include his response to a truly repentant people's prayers.

(5) Bible writers sometimes express God's actions in familiar human terms, without the intention of their readers' distorting the meaning. The modern term for this is anthropomorphism. Since we are far from understanding the dynamics of God's thinking and acting, we often speak in comparative language. We can hardly do anything else. Our ability to describe the nature, plans, revelations, actions, reactions and redemptive responses of God is paltry at best.

Chapter 12

The several references to Jacob the man, not the nation, in chapter 12 probably indicate the idea that the sins of Israel are rooted in part in the character of their forefather Jacob. The development of the character of his children and children's children was affected by the spirit and inclinations passed down from generation to generation.

Many students of the Bible believe that some families provide a continuing home not merely to their biological members, but also to various evil influences. It may be more defensible to say that demonic spirits find it easy to continue their influence in certain families where previous surrender to them has laid the groundwork for further exploitation.

In a similar way, of course, evidence would seem to indicate that God uses some families in holy ways, probably as much as anything because of the strong heritage of godly faith and surrender they build and leave to their successive generations. Whether unholy or holy, the pattern, if it exists, is merely a tendency or proclivity.

This may be the implication of the theme of chapter 12, where the LORD seems to be saying through Hosea that Jacob the nation is like Jacob of old.

1 **Ephraim feedeth on wind, and followeth after the east wind: he daily increaseth lies and desolation; and they do make a covenant with the Assyrians, and oil is carried into Egypt.**

The two expressions leading off this verse dealing with wind are ways of looking at the futility of Ephraim's hopes and the emptiness of her self-assurance. The reason is the national abandonment of Israel's calling to be a unique people and to worship Yahweh exclusively and from the heart. This fundamental spiritual rebellion and apostasy resulted in moral and ethical corruption of every kind; being disconnected from their internal source of righteousness left the people of Israel vulnerable to the grossest sort of temptations and allurements.

Desolation is elsewhere translated "violence" and probably should be here for contemporary understanding. **Lies** addresses civil injustices while **violence** countenances criminal acts.

On the national scene, Israel was attempting to stave off the increasingly certain future of foreign domination, by making treaties with the **Assyrians,** while they were increasing trade with **Egypt** hoping that their **olive oil** and other products would make that former captor less inclined to join Israel's enemies.

2   **The LORD hath also a controversy with Judah, and will punish Jacob according to his ways; according to his doings will he recompense him.**

Not forgetting the mounting iniquity of both kingdoms, Hosea says God's coming punishment will include **Judah,** and then he proceeds to unify the discipline as incorporating all of **Jacob,** the father of all the Israelites. What follows is an indictment of the *family*.

3   **He took his brother by the heel in the womb, and by his strength he had power with God.**

Going all the way back to the birth of the paterfamilias, Hosea recounts the birth of Jacob and Esau (Genesis 25:24-26). The purpose in this allusion to the history of their progenitor was to illustrate the national characteristic of **power with God.** The Genesis passage does not give us this interpretation of Jacob. In fact, Genesis 25:26 specifically says that the name Jacob was given to him because of the incident with his brother's heel. The name "Jacob" means "he grasps the heel," which became a Hebrew idiom for "deceives." The pattern appears several times in Jacob's subsequent life, sometimes augmented by the favoritism of his mother.

However, Hosea draws from Jacob's birth a parable of his power with God. He presents Jacob's heel-grasping as an act that prompted God's choice of him as the head of the people of divine choice instead of his first-born brother—or at least an act that elicited God's revelation of that choice. Jacob's later encounters were even more literal in their demonstration of this strength:

4 Yea, he had power over the angel, and prevailed: he wept, and made supplication unto him: he found him in Bethel, and there he spake with us.

The **angel** in this verse is the same as **God** in the previous verse. A careful study of Genesis 32:22ff shows without doubt that the "man" who wrestled with Jacob at Jabbok's ford, who called himself "God" (v28), was indeed a theophany of Yahweh himself. Elsewhere in numerous places referred to as the Angel of the LORD, this person—the same in every instance—was a pre-incarnation appearance of God the Son. While God the Father was never seen, God the Son revealed him to the patriarchs, judges, prophets and others (cp. John 1:18). In fact, the sense of direction and identity the patriarchs had, in a time when there was no *written* word of God, consisted largely of the divine word communicated through these appearances of the LORD. And because Jacob had shown the propensity for determined struggle to succeed, he earned the reputation for prevailing.

Jacob had a previous experience with the Lord at **Bethel** (Genesis 28) and then a later experience (Genesis 35) that personalized the call and promise given to his grandfather Abraham and then renewed that promise. In the latter encounter, Hosea says **there he spake with us**, indicating that the nation considered its relationship with God to emanate from its patriarchs and to consist of the same promises *to* them and the same commitments *from* them. When God spoke to Jacob, he was speaking to the nation that would come from him.

5 Even the LORD God of hosts; the LORD is his memorial.

Most translations take this verse to be an interjection, a sentence of praise in the midst of a historical recounting, elicited by the mention of the Lord's appearance and revelation. And if any doubt remains about the identity of the Angel of the Lord—in v4 and in the Genesis references—v5 positively identifies him as **the LORD of hosts.**

The word **memorial** in the KJV is translated elsewhere mostly as "name," even though the Hebrew *zikrow* means "memorial." Some translations supply "name" (ASV), or render the word "memorable name" (NKJV).

6   Therefore turn thou to thy God: keep mercy and judgment, and wait on thy God continually.

Most translators see **therefore** more as "but" or "so." The sense is that in view of Israel's heritage—but also *in spite of* it—they need to turn to God in order to be saved at this late hour. And that turning would have to be characterized by establishing and maintaining **mercy** (Hebrew *hesed,* "lovingkindness") and **judgment,** *(mispat,* "justice"), and also waiting on God *(qawweh).* This waiting is not inactivity, except as a total lack of guidance from God may imply the necessity of such. The Psalmist wrote that he waited on the Lord all day long (Psalm 25:5). He hardly meant he did nothing, in some anticipation of a divine appearance. As well as numerous instances where *qawweh* is rendered "wait," the same word is found in Jeremiah 8:15 and 14:19 where it means looking for something. This is the sense always implied. Waiting is not static: it is anticipatory and expectant. One who waits on the Lord goes on living by every obligation and purpose ever communicated by God in his word or in the verified leading of God's Spirit, while looking for further direction from God and not getting ahead of him by acting precipitously.

To sum up and paraphrase 11:12-12:6: The descendants of Jacob are unmanageable and undisciplined, inclined to trust anybody but God. Jacob started out life scrambling for position and became progressively more acquisitive, but finally he was broken and humbled by God in a close encounter with him. Similarly, the descendants of Jacob can change if they seek him and surrender to him.

7 He is a merchant, the balances of deceit are in his hand: he loveth to oppress.

The KJV has "merchant" the NKJV has "Canaanite," as do a few other minor translations. The difference in reading is due to the fact that the word Canaan had become a term for a trader or merchant because of the dominant occupation of these coastal peoples. But there was the association of dishonesty implicit in the term. To compare Israel with the Canaanites even in this way, however, was to criticize their character, as the rest of the verse makes more explicit: **the balances of deceit** are dishonest scales. Israelite merchants cheated their customers.

8 And Ephraim said, Yet I am become rich, I have found me out substance: in all my labours they shall find none iniquity in me that were sin.

I have found me out substance —I have become rich on my own terms. And in spite of the indictment of cheating, they put up a front of being entirely honest. They redefined their business practices as ethical, in the face of the plain word of God to the contrary.

9 And I that am the LORD thy God from the land of Egypt will yet make thee to dwell in tabernacles, as in the days of the solemn feast.

The Lord's answer to this boast is that they should recall the makeshift booths or lean-to's they lived in for a few days as part of the Feast of the Tabernacles, roughing it and recalling the difficult lives of their forebears: God was going to make them live in such rudimentary shelters full-time, when the nation was overrun by the enemy and carried off to Assyria. All this wealth they credited themselves for would be lost.

There is some difference of opinion about the reference to **tabernacles.** The Hebrew has *baohalim,* "in tents" and connects the word to **the solemn feast.** We take that as a reference to the Feast of the Tabernacles, which would have been the first event thought of when tabernacles were mentioned.

As a matter of application to the present, neither Israel nor any nation should think prosperity validates its fundamental way of life or protects it against disaster. God took Israel from its luxury and put it in tents again, and he can put any man or nation back in need and subservience, and without liberty.

10 I have also spoken by the prophets, and I have multiplied visions, and used similitudes, by the ministry of the prophets.

When the reversal of fortunes laid out in v9 comes about, it will not be for any lack of warning given to Israel. He has sent **prophets**, whose **visions** were clear and powerful as to the sin of the people. Through their **ministry** the northern kingdom had adequate notice.

The original language has *adammeh* for the KJV's "**ministry**,"which basically means "symbols." Most translations have "parables." Hosea's own ministry contained the very painful, living parable of his family's griefs, and other prophets told extensive parables or enacted them in the streets or in front of their houses in theatrical demonstrations.

11 Is there iniquity in Gilead? surely they are vanity: they sacrifice bullocks in Gilgal; yea, their altars are as heaps in the furrows of the fields.

In Hebrew the initial syllable *im* before Gilead can mean "though," or even "but," or it may simply turn the sentence into a question, as the Authorized Version has it. The sense is that in spite of the numerous ways God has tried to bring Israel to recognition of its sin and to repentance, the city centers of the country virtually broadcast the situation of the entire nation: worthless living (**vanity**) and idolatry are everywhere. Whether the **altars** in **heaps** in the **fields** is a picture of the countryside after Assyrian victory or a depiction of the sheer numbers of makeshift altars for idol worship everywhere one went, is a matter of opinion. The verb is not in the verse.

12 And Jacob fled into the country of Syria, and Israel served for a wife, and for a wife he kept sheep.

13 And by a prophet the LORD brought Israel out of Egypt, and by a prophet was he preserved.

These two verses are a little historical illustration, a call-to-remembrance of a well-known tale. The setting was the time of the patriarchs, when their ancestor Jacob was a young man still in his father Isaac's house.

Without recounting the fact that Jacob tricked his brother twice (at least) in significant matters and brought upon himself the necessity of running away from home, Hosea reminds the people of Israel that their distant grandfather had to flee for his life into Aram, which by Hosea's time was Syria (Hebrew *aram)*. In the description there is the understood presence and protection of God, who providentially led Jacob to a wife, oversaw his success in keeping sheep for Laban, and preserved him in his extraction from Laban's benevolent snares.

Still invoking the reverie of their common, cultural reverence for their extraordinary history, Hosea skips forward more than four hundred years, during which, as they knew, their forefathers were guests but then slaves in Egypt, and he reminds them that **the LORD** used a **prophet** (Moses) to bring them out of that country and to lead them for a generation in the wilderness, as they were being prepared to take the Promised Land. God had truly blessed and watched over them.

A subtle message is in these two verses in the words translated **he kept sheep,** and then, **he was preserved.** The root word in each case is *samar* - "kept." Jacob tried to escape settling down and he went and *kept* sheep. But God *kept* him by the prophet Moses. God has proven that despite extensive rebellion by Israel, he *kept* his promise.

Through this brief meditation on their holy history, Hosea sought to create a wistful flashback, but strategically he then demolishes any thoughts they might have of how blessed they are in the next verse:

14 **Ephraim provoked him to anger most bitterly: therefore shall he
    leave his blood upon him, and his reproach shall his Lord return
    unto him.**

    While the word is not there, "But" is the understood connector to
this thought. These descendants of the patriarchs so graciously led by
God, provided for in his bounty, and protected by his presence, have
provoked him mightily, as if not at all thankful for what he had done
for them for generations. **Blood** here is a complex word meaning the
(implied) guilt that comes upon someone for shedding blood. The root,
dam, appears many places, and in Leviticus 17:4 *(et al.)* it carries the
specific idea of transferrable guilt. **He** (the Lord) will leave **his**
(Ephraim's) blood guilt upon him, and let his (Ephraim's) shameful
conduct come back to bite him.

Chapter 13

Hosea 13 is another group of verses with flashback and then warnings of judgment. A possible glimmer of hope then appears, but is quickly obscured, the stubborn sinfulness of Israel erasing the proffered possibility of recovery.

1   **When Ephraim spake trembling, he exalted himself in Israel; but when he offended in Baal, he died.**

The original word for **trembling** was *retheth*. In the Hebrew, it is unclear whether Ephraim spoke trembling or when he spoke there *was* trembling. Considering that the next phrase says **he exalted himself**, it appears that the meaning is that Ephraim spoke trembling, or, in other words, he was humble or reserved. In result, he was **exalted** (Cp. Luke 14:11, 18:14). But once he (the ten tribes other than Benjamin and Judah) separated himself and began to take up Baal worship, **he died** —in the spiritual sense.

2   **And now they sin more and more, and have made them molten images of their silver, and idols according to their own understanding, all of it the work of the craftsmen: they say of them, Let the men that sacrifice kiss the calves.**

The point of saying the construction of the idols is **the work of the craftsman** is to emphasize how seriously they took their worship of Baals. These were no makeshift idols like figures of straw. A sizeable portion of their economy was taken up in the creation and sale of idol images and paraphernalia. That worshipers **kiss**ed the calf images was a demonstration of the deluded devotion they paid to these gods.

3   **Therefore they shall be as the morning cloud, and as the early dew that passeth away, as the chaff that is driven with the whirlwind out of the floor, and as the smoke out of the chimney.**

Four images depict Israel's soon dispersion into the peoples of their conquering countries, each one readily imagined. Their identity, their power, and their greatness would evaporate and fade away into the atmosphere of history. In a sense, these are the passive means of Israel's judgment. Although the initial conquest by Assyria would inaugurate it, the rest of the process would take place almost silently.

By contrast, the Lord's anger will have an active or aggressive quality as well, as outlined in vv4-9.

4 Yet I am the LORD thy God from the land of Egypt, and thou shalt know no god but me: for there is no saviour beside me.

Practically a restatement of the First Commandment, this declaration was intended to make anyone in Ephraim stop and think about the core of the nation's purpose. If—and only if—Israel would return to a life in which the LORD was their only God, then he would be savior as well.

5 I did know thee in the wilderness, in the land of great drought.

Again, Hosea injects a wistful reminder that even in places of trial and hardship, God knew them and provided for them. **I did know** is the same verb and form as in Jeremiah 1:5, where God knew that prophet even in the womb. In such passages as this one from Hosea's pen, that God knew his people says that he had fellowship with them on the basis of the most intimate knowledge of who and what they were, and his choice of them to belong to him.

6 According to their pasture, so were they filled; they were filled, and their heart was exalted; therefore have they forgotten me.

The picture is of Israel's progression from nothing to something; from something to more; from more to more than enough; and from more than enough to self-satisfaction and disinterest in the Lord who was with them and knew them when they had nothing.

7 Therefore I will be unto them as a lion: as a leopard by the way

will I observe them:

8   I will meet them as a bear that is bereaved of her whelps, and will
     rend the caul of their heart, and there will I devour them like a
     lion: the wild beast shall tear them.

As the "passive" judgments were multiplied in v3, here the "active"
judgments are represented in three commonly terrifying wild animals.
The **lion**, it is implied, surprises and attacks them; the **leopard** first
observes them, which would create mounting terror before the
inevitable; but the **bear**, whose cause of rage is known, sets upon them
with primal fury, and Hosea describes his gruesome mauling of the
victim. The mounting drama of these violent judgments is meant to
strike fear into Israel, as one of many means of penetrating their
irreverent and unholy hearts.

Verses 9-14 constitute a mixture of plea and warning. Some of the
difficult Hebrew passages of Hosea are in these verses.

9   O Israel, thou hast destroyed thyself; but in me is thine help.

The passive Hebrew is rendered active in some translations, as here
in the KJV, with the subject of **destroyed** being variously either God
or Israel itself. It is better to keep the passive, and infer the subject from
the following phrase, where God declares himself to be Israel's only
help. In fact, God will either destroy them or save them, depending
entirely upon whether Israel ignores his warnings or heeds them. In a
similar way, the same flood that destroyed the world bore Noah and his
family to a renewed world. God will not be *nothing* to any human being:
he will either be their Judge or their Savior.

10   I will be thy king: where is any other that may save thee in all thy
     cities? and thy judges of whom thou saidst, Give me a king and
     princes?

11   I gave thee a king in mine anger, and took him away in my wrath.

They were for all intents and purposes without a king—one of substantial power anyway, when Hosea addressed them. And they would be presently without one at all. Since this was so, the Lord presented himself to them again as their King, their Sovereign. None other than he could save them.

During the time of the judges Israel had looked around and had seen the other countries had kings, and they wanted one, too. God gave them one to show what it would be like. They reaped what they sowed, in the evils of the politics they chose over theocracy. Now by the word he gave to Hosea, God reminded them that he gave them a king and he could, as he did, take their kings away.

12 The iniquity of Ephraim is bound up; his sin is hid.

The root word behind **bound up** is *tsarar,* which has a component of "hostility" to it. The meaning here is not simply that Ephraim's iniquity is collected, but that it has been collected with the intent of its being released in an act of punishment. Likewise with his sins being **hid:** the root means to treasure up. The purpose is derived from the companion phrase: his sins are being treasured up for disposition in the form of wrath. Similarly, in Jeremiah 25:15, Psalm 75:8, Revelation 14:10 *et al.,* the cup of God's wrath is poured until full, and then released in judgment.

13 The sorrows of a travailing woman shall come upon him: he is an unwise son; for he should not stay long in the place of the breaking forth of children.

Childbirth should be thought of as ultimately a joyous event, but it involves the pain of labor and the possible danger of loss. In times past, that danger was far greater than in the modern era. Hosea creates an image of Israel as a child about to be born who decides not to come out. The picture doesn't make sense, which is precisely Hosea's point. Israel has a slim but real chance to **break forth**—be born again spiritually—if they will repent and return to the Lord, but the illustration implies that they have already delayed too long and will perish instead.

14 **I will ransom them from the power of the grave; I will redeem them from death: O death, I will be thy plagues; O grave, I will be thy destruction: repentance shall be hid from mine eyes.**

This one of the more difficult verses in the whole of Hosea to interpret. The Hebrew is not itself obscure, but questions exist as to whether interrogatives are meant in most or any of its phrases. And the interpretation of the entire verse is made the more difficult by the sense applied to it much later by the Apostle Paul when he quoted a portion of it in 1 Corinthians 15:55. Remembering that Paul was Saul of Tarsus, a highly educated Pharisaic Jew, it is well to give his interpretation due respect. That said, a caveat always exists against failing to interpret an Old Testament text in its own context.

Essentially, the verse is either (1) a sudden declaration of the Lord's great desire to heal and revive Israel, just as suddenly abandoned in v15; *or*, (2) it is a theoretical question about saving Israel, followed by a resolute refusal even to consider such.

Which interpretation the reader chooses rests on which phrases in the Hebrew he chooses to make into questions, if any.

The CSB (as well as NIV and ESV) takes the first two sentences to be firm statements, and the next two to be rhetorical questions:

I will ransom them from the power of Sheol. I will redeem them from death. Death, where are your barbs? Sheol, where is your sting? Compassion is hidden from my eyes (Hosea 13:14 CSB).

The NLT (as well as the CEV, and interestingly, the 1917 JPS Tanakh) takes the first two sentences to be questions, and the next two to be firm statements—negative answers to the questions:

> Should I ransom them from the grave? Should I redeem them
> from death? O death, bring on your terrors! O grave, bring on
> your plagues! For I will not take pity on them (Hosea 13:14
> NLT).

The other interpretive choice largely evades a unified interpretation in
that it takes all the Hebrew subject-verb combinations to be either
questions or statements, leaving the reader to determine how they relate
to each other. This was the approach of the KJV (and NKJV), and the
later Webster's Bible Translation.

Among the most interesting of translations of this verse is that of
the NET. It takes the first two phrases to be rhetorical questions,
supplying the answers, then takes the next two phrases to be
imperatives, and the last phrase to be declarative:

> Will I deliver them from the power of Sheol? No, I will not!
> Will I redeem them from death? No, I will not! O Death, bring
> on your plagues! O Sheol, bring on your destruction! My eyes
> will not show any compassion! (Hosea 13:14 NET).

The weakness of many of the versions is in the apparent disconnect
between the first four phrases/sentences and the final sentence. If a
note of hope is sounded by making the challenge to **death** and the
grave sound insurmountable, then leaving the final sentence as a
declarative statement vacates any hope thereby created.

But the powerful strength of the NET's interpretation lies in the
continuity of the thought of the entire verse.

What value, then, shall we give the interpretation of the Apostle
Paul? In essence, his quotation of the middle sentences of v14 was not
an interpretation of what Hosea meant when he wrote the words, but

rather a new meaning of Hosea's phraseology for the Christian era. For what seemed a hopeless condemnation—to be subjected to the **plagues** of **death** and the **destruction** of the **grave**—had become a new rhetorical question with the opposite answer: in Christ, death loses its sting and the grave loses its victory.

15 **Though he be fruitful among his brethren, an east wind shall come, the wind of the LORD shall come up from the wilderness, and his spring shall become dry, and his fountain shall be dried up: he shall spoil the treasure of all pleasant vessels.**

16 **Samaria shall become desolate; for she hath rebelled against her God: they shall fall by the sword: their infants shall be dashed in pieces, and their women with child shall be ripped up.**

The development of God's people thwarted and brought to a standstill by their own stubbornness, their phantom prosperity will be dissipated by the storm of God's rebuke. Their flimsy security will fall to economic disaster, and their assumption of physical safety will be rudely disproved.

These final verses of chapter 13 focus the coming judgment on the capital city of **Samaria** as representative of the country. The truly hideous images of soldiers killing **women with child** along with **their infants** adds an exclamation mark to the dire prophesies of the chapter.

Chapter 14

After the extended sermon of chapter 13 in which no stone of Israel's sin was left un-turned, finally there is an end to the exposition of evil and a conclusion filled with entreaty, the promise of salvation, the tenderness and goodness of God. Chapter 14 stands as God's invitation to repent and come back to the Lord wholeheartedly.

1   **O Israel, return unto the LORD thy God; for thou hast fallen by thine iniquity.**

The sum of the issue is that Israel's troubles and impending doom were solely the result of their sin, and the solution was wholehearted, thoroughgoing repentance. While political analysis might have yielded technical explanations for economic woes, international troubles and the approach of war, all of these things were the result of the sovereign intention or allowance of the Lord.

2   **Take with you words, and turn to the LORD: say unto him, Take away all iniquity, and receive us graciously: so will we render the calves of our lips.**

3   **Asshur shall not save us; we will not ride upon horses: neither will we say any more to the work of our hands, Ye are our gods: for in thee the fatherless findeth mercy.**

The Lord prescribed just how Israel was to return to him. They were to pray: to **take words**—very specific words indicating specific spiritual acts—the words had to be genuine and paired with obedience. Verses 2-3 lay out three steps to Israel's return:

(1) They were to confess their **iniquity** (*awon* - "guilt for iniquity"), and ask forgiveness (**take away**). Only if they were forgiven would their worship be received. **Render the calves of our lips** is a makeshift idiom for praise, since calves were the designated sacrifice and sacrifice represents praise and worship.

(2) They were to confess that their salvation lay neither in international treaties (**Asshur shall not save us**) nor military homeland

security (**we will not ride upon horses**), but only the Lord their God. In other words, in turning back to the Lord they would be abandoning any other reliance and confessing their total dependence on him.

(3) They were pointedly and emphatically to renounce any worship of, or tolerance of, other gods. This was the apex of their iniquity and had to be the focus of their repentance. Not in any "god" but only **in thee**—Yahweh—do the **fatherless** find mercy. The fatherless, or orphans, epitomize those who have no one to be their protector, teacher, guardian, and guide.

If Israel were to have turned back to the Lord in this way, even at such a late hour, the promise the prophet relayed to them would have held true:

4   **I will heal their backsliding, I will love them freely: for mine anger is turned away from him.**

5   **I will be as the dew unto Israel: he shall grow as the lily, and cast forth his roots as Lebanon.**

6   **His branches shall spread, and his beauty shall be as the olive tree, and his smell as Lebanon.**

7   **They that dwell under his shadow shall return; they shall revive as the corn, and grow as the vine: the scent thereof shall be as the wine of Lebanon.**

As there were three specific steps to Israel's repentance, God's blessings, as Hosea summed them up, would also be three:

(1) He would forgive their sin and change their hearts so they would be faithful to him rather than rebellious (**heal their backsliding**). A host of versions render the Hebrew for **backsliding** as "apostasy." The modern sense given to "backsliding" is far too minor to communicate what the original language indicated.

(2) He would express his love for them rather than his wrath (**love them freely**). (See above on 13:9.)

(3) He would restore their joy, fruitfulness, and renown. The

horticultural images of vv5-7 symbolize these interpersonal and national blessings. The "economic sanctions" imposed by the Lord would be lifted.

It is possible that the **smell as Lebanon** (v6) was the powerful and pleasant smell of cedar, for which Lebanon was known. Refer to the description of the building of Solomon's palace in 1 Kings 7, especially v7, where the throne hall was covered from floor to ceiling in cedar.

While the message of Hosea was not designed primarily to look far into the future at messianic blessings, it is not difficult to apply the principles of 14:1-7 to the gospel proclamation of the New Testament era. Confession of sin, true and thorough repentance, and trust in the grace of God—ultimately in Jesus the Messiah—result in forgiveness, restoration, and spiritual rebirth. However, these requisites and results were always the steps to approaching God before, and always shall be.

Almost as a postscript, the response of Ephraim *would have been* something like what Hosea adds as an echo of God's restorative work:

8   **Ephraim shall say, What have I to do any more with idols? I have heard him, and observed him: I am like a green fir tree. From me is thy fruit found.**

With too few words in the original to determine who is speaking, the first phrase of v8 is sometimes put in the mouth of Ephraim and sometimes in the mouth of God. The LXX is not helpful in determining which was meant. We think more sense is made by regarding the words as the hopeful, future words of Ephraim/Israel. In this interpretation, Ephraim the nation is depicted as one man, being looked at through the lens of history, who speaks of his life post-repentance, amidst revival, vowing to worship the Lord God alone, always.

What would be God's answer to this eventual vow of absolute fealty by Ephraim in future? God hears and sees him (**heard…observed**). These simple words (*anah,* "heard"; and *sur,* - "seen") have been taken to mean "answer prayers" and "watch over," or some such derivative ideas. This may well be the implied meaning. However, the two words may be a brief way of suggesting that God heard what they said and saw their repentance and was watching to see if they would follow through. If they did, they would find that he was like a **green fir tree** —the Hebrew suggests cypress, but others take it to be an almond tree—and if they are like branches from the ever-living God, they will produce **fruit.** The fruit God wants from his people consists of righteous living, love for one another, faithfulness in the doing of his will, and success in being his kingdom's representatives as the chosen people of history.

To all the foregoing promises—both Ephraim's and God's—Hosea adds this conclusion of appeal and caution:

9   **Who is wise, and he shall understand these things? prudent, and he shall know them? for the ways of the LORD are right, and the just shall walk in them: but the transgressors shall fall therein.**

Much like the pithier warning and advice in Revelation 2:7, "He that hath an ear, let him hear what the Spirit saith…", this verse advises the **wise** and **prudent** to take in everything the prophet wrote and act on every command and invitation of the Lord. Then in a historically very Jewish manner the prophecy closes not only with the promise of blessing but also with a note of eternal warning: those who are deemed righteous will be those who **walk** in the **ways of the Lord,** but those who are found at last to be unrighteous (**transgressors**) will be those who tripped up over *the same commands* of the Lord that the righteous obeyed. In other words, they rebelled against the word of God, rejected his Lordship, and refused his fellowship. The fundamental divide among human beings is whether they regard, believe, and obey the word of God, or else disregard, reject, and disobey him. For in the end it is not merely reasonably good living—as they define it themselves—God wants from human beings, but faith, worship and fellowship.

www.ingramcontent.com/pod-product-compliance
Lightning Source LLC
Chambersburg PA
CBHW070942150426
42812CB00066B/3219/J